KB270088

# Arirang Korean Basics 1

# Arirang Korean Basics 1


| | |
|---|---|
| **Written by** | Language Education Institute, Seoul National University |
| **Translated by** | Peter Schroepfer |

| | |
|---|---|
| **First Published** | November, 2006 |
| **5th Printing** | August, 2012 |
| **Publisher** | Chung Kyudo |
| **Editor** | Lee Sukhee, Lee Eunju, Jang Byungsik |
| **Designer** | Son Hyejung, Choi Youngran |

**DARAKWON** Published by Darakwon Inc.
211 Munbal-ro, Paju-si, Gyeonggi-do, Republic of Korea 413-756
Tel : 02-736-2031  Fax : 02-732-2037
(Marketing Dept. ext.: 113,114  Editorial Dept. ext.: 201~204)




**Price : 12,000 won (with Audio CD)**


ISBN :  978-89-5995-760-6 18710
        978-89-5995-757-6 (set)


**http://www.darakwon.co.kr**
**http://www.darakwon.co.kr/koreanbooks**

※ Visit the Darakwon homepage to learn about our other publications and promotions, and
  to download the contents of the CD in MP3 format.

# Arirang Korean Basics 1

서울대학교 언어교육원
Language Education Institute, Seoul National University

DARAKWON

## : 서문

이 책은 한국어를 배우고자 하는 성인 한국어 학습자를 대상으로 한 한국어 교재로, 특별히 Arirang TV에서 방송되는 Let's Speak Korean을 통해 한국어를 배우는 사람들의 이해를 돕고 나아가서는 방송을 시청하지 않지만 살아 있는 한국어 말하기 표현을 배우고자 하는 한국어 학습자를 위해 편찬한 것이다.

이 책은 의사소통적 언어 교수법을 근간으로 하여 문법은 되도록 기능적 범주에 스며들어 부각되지 않도록 제공하였다. '대화' 속에서 오늘의 문법이 자연스럽게 도출되도록 하였고 문법 설명을 최소화시키는 대신 내용과 상황에 대한 이해와 구문의 활용에 중점을 두었다. 또한 '유창성' 부분에 초점을 맞추어 진정성 있는 언어를 많이 사용함으로써 대화의 부자연스러움을 탈피하고자 하였다.

이 책은 다음의 몇 가지 특징을 가진다.

**쉽다** 이 책은 한국어 자모만 읽을 수 있으면 누구나 쉽게 한국어 구문을 익힐 수 있도록 쉬우면서도 바로 실생활에서 사용 가능한 구문들을 엄선하여 제공하였다.

**재미있다** 이 책은 문법을 가르치기 위한 대화를 제공했던 전통적인 언어 교재와는 달리 실제 생활에서 많이 들을 수 있는 구문과 쉽고 재미있는 내용들로 구성하였다.

**간단하다** 이 책은 전체 구성면에서뿐만 아니라 내용 기술면에서 되도록 짧고 간결하게 구성하여 자칫 지루해지기 쉬운 언어 학습의 단점을 피하고자 하였다. 그러나 핵심 내용은 간결하면서도 명료하게 설명하여 애매한 부분이 발생하지 않도록 노력하였다.

**진정성(Authenticity)이 있다** 대화 부분은 어색함이 없는 살아 있는 한국어 구문을 엄선하였으며 이러한 점은 학습자들의 언어 학습 동기를 자극하는데도 많은 도움을 줄 것이다. 또한 문화 부분에서도 지금까지 한국어 교재에서는 제대로 다루지 않은, 실생활의 아주 작은 부분까지 다룸으로써 학습자로 하여금 문화라는 것이 실제 언어생활 속에 스며들어 있는 것임을 느끼고 이해할 수 있도록 하였다.

이 책이 완성되기까지 많은 분들의 헌신적인 도움이 있었다. 이 책의 번역을 맡아 주신 서반석 선생님, 서울대학교 언어교육원의 홍기선 원장님, 아리랑 방송의 장명호 사장님, 그리고 이 책의 출판을 맡아 주신 다락원 정효섭 회장님과 편집진 여러분께 감사의 마음을 전한다.

김은애, 김은영

# : Introduction

Arirang Korean Basics was written for adult learners of the Korean language. First and foremost it was designed to be your companion while watching the Arirang TV program "Let's Speak Korean," but it is our hope that it will also be useful to readers who, sadly enough, are not able to view the program.

Methodologically speaking, Arirang Korean Basics is based on the communicative language approach, and we did our best avoid overemphasizing grammar, keeping it as something taught in context.

This book has four main characteristics.

**It's easy.** Functional expressions for the actual situations of everyday life were carefully chosen and are explained in a way that allows anyone who knows Korean characters to learn Korean sentence constructions with ease.

**It's fun.** The traditional Korean textbook gave you dialogue that centered around the teaching of grammar. Arirang Korean Basics gives you fun and easy expressions applicable in real life.

**It's simple.** We wrote Arirang Korean Basics in a way that keeps things simple in terms of overall composition and content, by avoiding the pitfalls that often make learning languages a bore. We made things clear and simple so that you will not run into areas that are too vague for you to understand.

**The dialogues are real.** There is nothing awkward about the dialogues you will find in Arirang Korean Basics, because we chose them for being real and they will be encourage you to study harder. The sections about Korean culture found in each chapter cover the smallest details of real Korean life, and were created to help students feel and understand how culture permeates language.

We received generous assistance in the course of writing Arirang Korean Basics. We express our thanks to translator, Seo Banseok (Peter Schroepfer); Director Hong Kiseon of Seoul National University's Language Education Institute; Chang Myungho, president of Arirang TV; and to Chung Hyosup, chairman of the publisher Darakwon and the Darakwon editorial staffs for making this book.

Kim Eunae, Kim Eunyoung

Arirang Korean Basics 1 was written as your companion to the Arirang TV program Korean language learning program "Let's Speak Korean." Each chapter has been organized into the following sections: Dialogue, Vocabulary & Expressions, Grammar Focus, Practice, More Expressions, and Korean Insight.

In "**Dialogue**" sections you will find the conversations discussed in each broadcast. Use this section to prepare and review for each program. Each Dialogue section has a "Pronunciation Check" sidebar, which will help you with potential tricky points in pronunciation. "Vocabulary & Expressions" sections are where you will find the vocabulary and expressions you will need for each section, so that you can study the lesson at hand and do not have to keep turning to a dictionary.

"**Grammar Focus**" sections provide you with just the right amount of grammar and vocabulary information you need to fully appreciate the lesson discussed in each "Let's Speak Korean" broadcast, but with as many practical examples as possible. When detailed explanations are required, look for the star ("★"), where you will see friendly talk about points that are potentially hard or confusing.

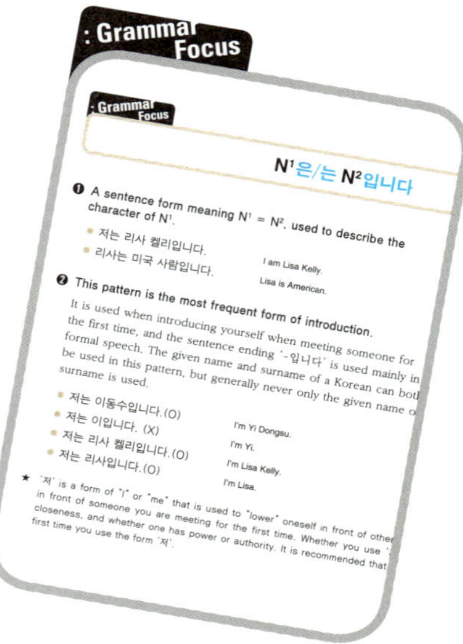

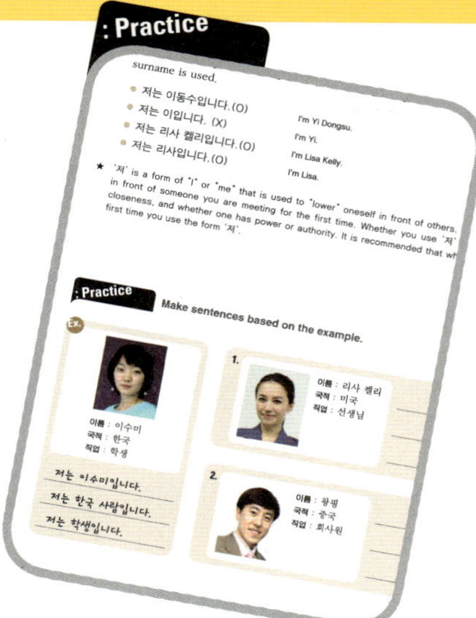

Each chapter's "**Practice**" section provides you with the practice you need to get the gist of the lesson's grammar, vocabulary, and expression points. There will be times when the television program's quiz section goes by too fast for comfort; it is in the Practice section of Arirang Korean Basics 1 that you will find what you need to review following the broadcast.

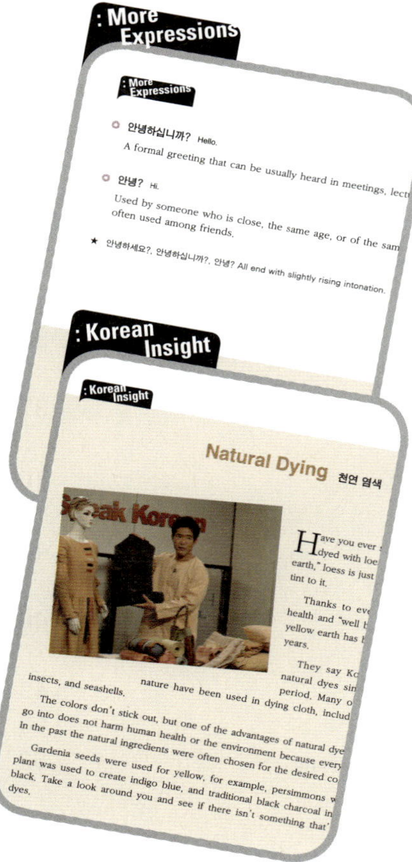

The "**More Expressions**" section gives you useful expressions related to the days lesson but not discussed on air. Study these expressions in addition to the dialogues you see on "Let's Speak Korean" and you will see your ability to converse in Korean grow in ways you will appreciate in daily life.

The "**Korean Insight**" section in each chapter gives you additional information about Korean culture. Knowing more about Korean culture will help you speak Korean all the better, right? If you watch the culture-related footage on the television program and then read the corresponding section in Arirang Korean Basics 1, you will learn a lot about the culture of Korea in the process.

# : Contents

: **Contents**

## Appendix

# : Table of Contents

Your companion to Let's Speak Korean on arirang TV

Now, how about starting
your exciting study of
the Korean language
with Arirang Korean Basics 1?

# 안녕하세요?

Hello.

Track
001

: Dialogue

A 안녕하세요? 리사 켈리입니다.

B 반갑습니다. 저는 김영입니다.

A Hello, I am Lisa Kelly.

B Nice to meet you. I am Kim Young.

**안녕하세요? Hello.**

When people meet in Korea they say "안녕하세요." without regard to whether it is morning or afternoon.

---

**: Pronunciation Check**

입니다 [임니다]　　반갑습니다 [반갑씀니다]

**: Vocabulary & Expressions**

| | | | |
|---|---|---|---|
| 저 I/me | 나 I/me | 이름 name | 국적 nationality |
| 직업 occupation, job | 한국 Korea | 미국 the United States | 중국 China |
| 한국 사람 Korean | 미국 사람 American | 중국 사람 Chinese | 학생 student |
| 선생님 teacher | 회사원 company employee | | |
| 안녕하세요? Hello. | 반갑습니다. Nice to meet you. | | |

# N¹은/는 N²입니다

**❶ A sentence form meaning N¹ = N², used to describe the character of N¹.**

- 저는 리사 켈리입니다.  I am Lisa Kelly.
- 리사는 미국 사람입니다.  Lisa is American.

**❷ This pattern is the most frequent form of introduction.**

It is used when introducing yourself when meeting someone for the first time, and the sentence ending '-입니다' is used mainly in formal speech. The given name and surname of a Korean can both be used in this pattern, but generally never only the given name or surname is used.

- 저는 이동수입니다.(O)  I'm Yi Dongsu.
- 저는 이입니다. (X)  I'm Yi.
- 저는 리사 켈리입니다.(O)  I'm Lisa Kelly.
- 저는 리사입니다.(O)  I'm Lisa.

★ '저' is a form of "I" or "me" that is used to "lower" oneself in front of others. You do not "elevate" yourself in front of someone you are meeting for the first time. Whether you use '저' or '나' is determined by age, closeness, and whether one has power or authority. It is recommended that when you meet someone for the first time you use the form '저'.

**은/는**

Korean requires a "subject particle" after the subject of a sentence. If the last syllable in a subject noun is a consonant, use the subject particle form '은'. If it ends in a vowel, use the form '는'.

Ex. 저**는**, 선생님**은**



**Make sentences, based on the example.**

**Ex.**

이름 : 이수미
국적 : 한국
직업 : 학생

저는 이수미입니다.

저는 한국 사람입니다.

저는 학생입니다.

**1.**

이름 : 리사 켈리
국적 : 미국
직업 : 선생님

**2.**

이름 : 왕핑
국적 : 중국
직업 : 회사원

- **안녕하십니까?** Hello.

  A formal greeting that can be usually heard in meetings, lectures, and on television news.

- **안녕?** Hi.

  Used by someone who is close, the same age, or of the same or greater social status. It is often used among friends.

★ 안녕하세요?, 안녕하십니까?, 안녕? All end with slightly rising intonation.

# Natural Dying 천연 염색

Have you ever seen clothes or underwear dyed with loess? Also known as "yellow earth," loess is just dirt that has a yellow tint to it.

Thanks to ever-increasing interest in health and "well being," clothing dyed with yellow earth has been selling well in recent years.

They say Koreans have been using natural dyes since the Three Kingdoms period. Many of the things you find in nature have been used in dying cloth, including flowers, grass, earth, insects, and seashells.

The colors don't stick out, but one of the advantages of natural dyes is that the clothing they go into does not harm human health or the environment because everything comes from nature. In the past the natural ingredients were often chosen for the desired color.

Gardenia seeds were used for yellow, for example, persimmons were used for red, indigo plant was used to create indigo blue, and traditional black charcoal ink was used for the color black. Take a look around you and see if there isn't something that's been dyed with natural dyes.

# 제 친구입니다.

## This is my friend.

Track
002

**A** 제 친구 리사입니다.

**B** 안녕하세요? 김영입니다.
처음 뵙겠습니다.

A   This is my friend Lisa.
B   Hello. I'm Kim Young. Nice to meet you.

**처음 뵙겠습니다.**
**Nice to meet you.**

This means that I meet you for the first time. This expression is used in Korea when two people first introduce themselves, much like "I'm pleased to meet you." It is a very formal greeting.

**: Pronunciation Check**

뵙겠습니다 [뵙껟씀니다]

**: Vocabulary & Expressions**

| | | |
|---|---|---|
| 제 my, mine (formal) | 친구 friend | 처음 first, beginning |
| 뵙다 to meet, see (honorific form) | 동생 younger sibling | 가방 bag, pack |
| 우산 umbrella | 책상 desk | 책 book |
| 다음에 next (time) | | |

## N¹의 N²

Used to express possession. He who is in possession of N² fills the spot N¹.

- 제 친구입니다.　　　　　　My friend.
- 제 동생입니다.　　　　　　My younger sibling.
- 리사의 가방입니다.　　　　Lisa's bag.

★ '저의' can be shortened to '제' and, similarly, '나의' can be shortened to '내'. Note that all of these must be followed by a noun.

- 저의 친구 / 제 친구　　　　My friend.
   → Be careful : '저의' is pronounced as if written '저에[저에]' and '나의' as if '나에[나에]'.

★ '제' can be either the nominative case or possessive case, but today we will practice only the possessive form.

## 뵙다

The word '뵙다' is honorific for '보다'. Use it with someone with whom you should use the honorific form.

- 처음 뵙겠습니다.　　　　Nice to meet you. (lit. "We meet for the first time.")

 **Make sentences based on the example. The following are the belongings of Lisa and Kim Young. Both would like to inform their friends of which item belongs to**

김영 : 제 책입니다.

1. 리사 : _______________
2. 토미 : _______________
3. 왕핑 : _______________

- **다음에 또 뵙겠습니다.**  See you again, next time.

  A formal expression used when parting, spoken towards someone with whom you need to use honorific language.

- **다음에 찾아 뵙겠습니다.**  I will visit you at the next opportunity.

  Say this to someone with whom you must use honorific language, to tell him you are unable to call on someone at the moment, so will visit at a later date.

: Korean Insight

# Kkakdugi  깍두기

Have you ever tasted Korean kimchi? It is easy to think of only the variety made from cabbage, but there are actually many different types of kimchi.

"kkakdugi" is famous one of kimchi, and made from radish. It has a hexahedral shape and you can be sure to have some if you eat at a restaurant specializing in galbitang or samgyetang.

It has been eaten for around 200 years, since back during the Joseon period. They say it was especially popular in winter, when it's hard to grow cabbage, and that people used to mix fish with kkakdugi when they made it. It isn't as hard to make as regular kimchi, so why don't you try to make some at home?

# 내일 만나요.
## See (you) tomorrow.

A  내일 만나요.
B  네, 안녕히 가세요.

A  See (you) tomorrow. / Let's meet tomorrow.
B  Yes, goodbye.

**Dialogue Tips**

**안녕히 가세요.**
Goodbye.

Said to someone who is departing by person who will stay behind.

**네.** Yes.

'네' has many meanings. Here it means one is okay.

**안녕히 가세요** [안녕히가세요]*
*Here the "ㅎ" gets pronounced softly.

| | | |
|---|---|---|
| 내일 tomorrow | 만나다 to meet | 가다 to go |
| 보다 to see | 공부하다 to study | 오다 to come |
| 먹다 to eat | 마시다 to drink | 배우다 to learn |
| 운전하다 to drive | 안녕히 가세요. Goodbye. (said to person staying) | |
| 안녕히 계세요. Goodbye. (said by person leaving) | | |

# V-아/어요

An informal present tense sentence ending. Used with someone with whom you are acquainted.

- 다음에 또 봐요. — See you later.
- 같이 공부해요. — Let's study together.

❶ If the stem of the syllable ends with 'ㅏ' or 'ㅗ', it becomes '-아요'.

- 가다      가 + 아요 → 가요
- 오다      오 + 아요 → 와요

❷ If the stem of the syllable ends with '-하다', the '하' of '-하다' verbs becomes '해' to form '해요'.

- 공부하다 → 공부해요

❸ In all other instances, this ending is '-어요'.

- 먹다      먹 + 어요 → 먹어요
- 마시다      마시 + 어요 → 마셔요
- 배우다      배우 + 어요 → 배워요

 Make sentences using today's sentence ending with the verbs below, based on the example.

**Ex.**

만나다 → <u>만나요.</u>

1. 가다 → ________________
2. 오다 → ________________
3. 먹다 → ________________
4. 보다 → ________________

5. 마시다 → ________________
6. 배우다 → ________________
7. 공부하다 → ________________
8. 운전하다 → ________________

○ **안녕히 계세요.** Goodbye.

Said by the person leaving to the person staying.

○ **다음에 봐요.** See you later. See you next time.

This means the same as "다음에 만나요."

○ **또 봐요.** See you again.

This means the same as "또 만나요."

○ **잘 가요.** Bye.

A casual expression used when parting.



# Yogang 요강

Do you know what a "yogang" is? Put simply, it's a portable toilet. Once upon a time Korean homes did not have restrooms in the same structure, so they were built separate from the buildng.

That meant that in bad weather or when it was cold, going to the restroom was an uncomfortable affair.

That is what led to the use of yogang, the portable toilet, widely used by commoners and the aristocratic class from as early as the Baekje period. Brides brought them to their new homes as wedding gifts.

They were often made of brass, albata, or china and were made to function aesthetically as well, and so were usually decorated with designs on their surfaces. Yogang used by men and women differed in shape, and you could tell a lot about a household's social and economic status by the quality of its yogangs. Almost no one uses them anymore, but you can still find them easily enough in antique stores. Foreigners find them quite amusing.

# 여기는 방이에요.
This is the room.

**A** 여기는 리사 씨 방이에요.
**B** 저기는 화장실이에요.

A This ("here") is Lisa's room.
B That is the restroom.

**Dialogue Tips**

**여기** here, this
Indicates a location close to the speaker.

**저기** there, that
Indicates a location far from both the speaker and the hearer.

**거기** there, that
Indicates a location close to the hearer, or a place not visible but known to both parties.

**화장실이에요** [화장시리에요]

| | | | |
|---|---|---|---|
| 여기 here, this | 방 room | 저기 there, that | 화장실 restroom |
| 병원 clinic, hospital | 은행 bank | 백화점 department store | |

# N이에요

An informal form of 'N입니다', used when the final syllable ends in a consonant.

- 여기는 병원이에요.  This is a hospital.
- 저기는 은행이에요.  That (over there) is a bank.
- 여기는 방이에요.  This is a (bed) room.
- 거기는 화장실이에요.  That's a restroom.
- 거기는 방이에요?  Is that a (bed)room?
- 저는 학생이에요.  I am a student.

★ The interrogative form of 'N이에요' is 'N이에요?', and the interrogative form of 'N입니다' is 'N입니까?'.

★ The negative form of 'N이에요' is 'N이/가 아니에요'. In a formal sentence, 'N이/가 아닙니다' has to be said.

- 여기는 방이에요?  Is here a room?
- 여기는 방이 아닙니다.  Here is not a room.

 **Make sentences, based on the example.**

| Ex. | 여기, 방 → | 여기는 방이에요. |

| | | |
|---|---|---|
| 1. | 저기, 화장실 → | |
| 2. | 여기, 은행 → | |
| 3. | 거기, 병원 → | |
| 4. | 저, 학생 → | |
| 5. | 리사, 미국 사람 → | |
| 6. | 왕핑, 회사원 → | |

- 네. / 아니요.  Yes. / No.

- A : 여기는 병원이에요?  Is this a hospital?
  B : 네, 병원이에요.  Yes, it's a hospital.

- A : 저기는 은행이에요?  Is that a bank?
  B : 아니요, 백화점이에요.  No, it's a department store.



# Jindogae (Jindo Dog)  진돗개

Jindo, or "Jin Island," located in South Jeolla province, is home to the "jindogae," a designated natural treasure. This species of dog receive special government protection.

In order to preserve the bloodline and maintain the species, each has a special chip placed in its body as soon as it is born in order to keep track of them, and you need to have a government permit to remove one from the island. Most jindogae fall into five categories, according to appearance; "yellow dog" (hwanggu, 황구), "white dog" (baekgu, 백구), "gray dog" (jaegu, 재구), "tiger dog" (hogu, 호구), and "four-eyed dog" (nenunbagi, 네눈박이). In very rare cases you can find jindogae that are more reddish than yellow, or that have alternating colors like a baduk board.

Jindogae are famous for being highly active and thoroughly faithful to their owners. There are many touching stories about them, like when one was found next to its owner five days after the owner had died, or about one that crossed several provinces to find its way home. It is a Korean dog, one well loved for its courage and strength despite its small size, and for its intelligence.

# 슈퍼가 어디예요?
## Where's the supermarket?

Track
005

**A** 슈퍼가 어디예요?
**B** 저기예요.
**A** 고맙습니다.

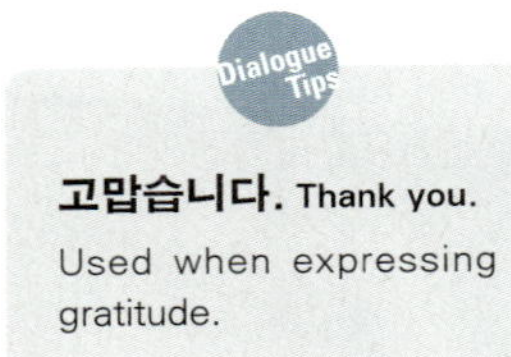
**고맙습니다.** Thank you.
Used when expressing gratitude.

A   Where's the supermarket?
B   Over there.
A   Thank you.

**: Pronunciation** Check
고맙습니다 [고맙씀니다]

**: Vocabulary & Expressions**

| | | |
|---|---|---|
| 슈퍼 supermarket | 어디 where | 학교 school |
| 도서관 library | 식당 restaurant | 집 house, home |
| 교회 church | 고맙습니다. Thank you. | |

# N예요

An informal form of the expression 'N입니다', used when the last syllable of N is a vowel. The interrogative form is 'N예요?'.

- 리사예요.     (I'm) Lisa.
- 어디예요?     Where is it? / Where are you?
- 저기예요.     Over there.
- 학교예요.     This is a school.

★ When N's final syllable ends in a consonant, use the sentence ending '이에요'. (See Unit 4)

- 도서관이에요.     This is a library.
- 식당이에요.     That's a restaurant.

★ The negative form of 'N예요/이에요' is 'N이/가 아니에요'.

- 학교가 아니에요.     That's not a school.
- 도서관이 아니에요.     This is not a library.

**이/가**

In Korean sentences the subject is followed by a subject particle. If the last syllable in a noun ends in a consonant, use the subject particle '이'. If it ends in a vowel, use the subject particle '가'.

Ex. 슈퍼**가**, 학교**가**
     화장실**이**, 은행**이**

## Practice

**Make sentences, based on the example.**

- **감사합니다.**  Thank you.

  The same as "고맙습니다." Use it with the formal sentence ending.

- **고마워.**  Thanks.

  Use this only with a very close friend or someone younger than yourself.

- **슈퍼가 어디에 있어요?**  Where is the supermarket?

  Use this expression when you ask the location of the market. "슈퍼가 어디예요?" has the same meaning.



# King Sejong 세종대왕

Can you identify the person on the 10,000 won Korean bill? It's none other than King Sejong, the man who created the Korean alphabet, hangeul. Sejong was the third king of the Joseon Dynasty, and was respected for running the country well.

It would be safe to say that the period of his reign was the best time in history as far as culture and government were concerned. The writing system he created is recognized as being a particularly systematic one.

Korea did not have a writing system adequate for the Korean language, so up until one point Chinese characters were Korea's writing system, which, because of the difficulty of learning Chinese, meant that most people were unable to read and write. Sejong is said to have decided to create an alphabet for Korean out of his love for his subjects. Nowadays Korean ranks as the twelfth most spoken language on the planet. Shouldn't we feel a sense of gratitude to King Sejong every time we speak Korean?

# 우유 있어요?
Do you have milk?

**: Dialogue**

A   어서 오세요.

B   우유 있어요?

A   네, 있어요.

A   Welcome!

B   Do you have milk?

A   Yes, we do.

**Dialogue Tips**

**어서 오세요.**   Welcome.
Said by employees in stores and restaurants to welcome customers. The more formal "어서 오십시오." can also be heard with some frequency.

---

**: Pronunciation Check**    있어요 [이써요]

---

**: Vocabulary & Expressions**

| | | |
|---|---|---|
| 우유 milk | 빵 bread | 초콜릿 chocolate |
| 사과 apple | 물 water | 김밥 gimbap |
| 있어요 is, I/we have | 없어요 is not, I/we don't have | |

어서 오세요. Welcome. (lit. "come quickly")

# N 있어요?

An ending used as a question, to ascertain the existence of something. Usually it is 'N 이/가 있어요?', but it can also be said 'N 있어요?' in colloquial speech.

- 리사 있어요?          Is Lisa there?
- 우유 있어요?          Do you have milk?

- A : 빵 있어요?          Do you have bread?
  B : 아니요, 없어요.          No, I don't.

★ Most often, '있어요' does not itself get turned into a negative form. Instead, the antonymous form '없어요' is used to express the opposite of '있어요'.

★ When finding someone who is older or in a higher position, use '(김 선생님, 사장님) 계세요?' instead of '있어요'. Also, as a negative response to the question, '안계세요' can be appropriate .



Here you see a list of items in a store. Ask and answer questions, based on the example, by referring to the list.

List :  빵,          초콜릿,          물,          사과

**Ex.**

A : 빵 있어요?
B : 네, 있어요.

A : 김밥 있어요?
B : 아니요, 없어요.

**1.**

A : _______________

B : _______________

**2.**

A : _______________

B : _______________

**3.**

A : _______________

B : _______________

- **다음에 또 오세요.**  Please come again next time.

  Used by store and restaurant employees to a departing customer.

- **저쪽에 있어요. / 저기에 있어요.**  It's over there.

  An employee will say this to a customer to tell him a given item is located somewhere that is close to neither of them.

- **뭐 찾으세요?**  What are you looking for? / Are you looking for something?

  A store employee will ask this of a customer to ask him if he needs help or to find out what he has come to purchase.



# Hanji Craftwork 한지공예

Do you know what "hanji" is? Hanji is paper made through traditional Korean involving the boiling and drying of tree bark. It is very soft to the touch yet is not torn easily, and it is very suitable for traditional calligraphy or painting because it holds ink well.

In the old days it was even used instead of cotton to fill clothes and make them warm, and some types of hanji were strong enough to be worn as clothing. It was also used to make gifts each member of a couple might give to the new household in marriage, like decorative boxes, workbaskets, meal cloths, and so on.

Artisans specializing in the making of articles from hanji used to make things to order or sell them in markets. It is amazing that people made crafts from paper? Hanji carries with it the tradition of Korea. That's probably what makes it look all the more special.

* Photograph copyright 2005 (www.ohmyhanji.com). Used with permission.

# 어디 있어요?

Where is it?

A  어디 있어요?

B  오른쪽에 있어요.

A  Where is it?
B  To (the/your) right.

**어디 있어요?**
**Where is it?**
Used when inquiring about the whereabouts of an object or person.

**: Pronunciation Check**　　오른쪽에 [오른쪼게]

**: Vocabulary & Expressions**

| | | | |
|---|---|---|---|
| 오른쪽 right (side) | 에 in, at | 왼쪽 left (side) | 위 above, on |
| 아래 under | 의자 chair | 앞 front | 뒤 back, behind |
| 시계 clock | 옆 next | 상자 box | |

# N에 있어요

An expression used when informing someone of the location of a thing or person. The question form is "있어요?" The particle '에' is usually omitted from the question form in colloquial speech.

- 책상 **위**에 있어요.  It is on the desk.  

- 책상 **아래**에 있어요.  It is under the desk.  

- 의자 **앞**에 있어요.  It is in front of the chair.  

- 의자 **뒤**에 있어요.  It is behind the chair.  

- 시계 **옆**에 있어요.  It is next to the clock.  

 **Complete the dialogues, based on the example.**

Ex.

A : 사과 __어디 있어요?__

B : 상자 __앞에 있어요.__

1.

A : 우유 _______________

B : 상자 _______________

2.

A : 시계 _______________

B : 상자 _______________

○ **A : 어디 있어요?**   Where is (it/he/she)?

**B : 잘 모르겠는데요.**   I don't know.

An expression for when one does not know the answer to a question about the location of a thing or a person.

○ **따라 오세요.**   Follow me. (Come this way.)

Used by a store employee when assisting a customer.



## Korean Break Dancers 한국의 비보이

Have you heard about "B-Boys?" The term refers to someone who does "break dancing." Women who break dance are called "B-Girls." These are people known as "street dancers" and their dance is known around the world as a new cultural and sports phenomenon. Break dancing is about young people improvising as they dance, but B-Boys make their performance in coordination with each other, which can only be done after long hours of practice.

There has been a lot of interest in B-Boys in Korea ever since young Korean B-Boys won the world championship. Lately they have been appearing in television advertisements, dramas, and musicals.

The reason they have been welcomed with such a warm response from the Korean public might be that they inherit the spirit of cooperation so valued by our ancestors. How about losing yourself in a cool performance by Korean B-Boys?

# 008

# 이거 얼마예요?

How much is this?

Track
008

**A** 이거 얼마예요?

**B** 천 원이에요.

A How much is this?
B One thousand won.

Dialogue Tips

**얼마예요? / 얼마입니까?**
**How much is this?**

Expression used to ask the price of something.

**이거 얼마예요?**
**How much is this?**

When saying "이거," you are usually pointing at something with your finger.

---

천 원이에요 [처눠니에요]

| | | | |
|---|---|---|---|
| 이거 this | 얼마 how much | 원 won (the Korean currency) | 수박 watermelon |
| 일 one | 오 five | 십 ten | 백 a hundred |
| 천 a thousand | 만 ten thousand | 얼마예요? How much is it/this? | |

# N이/가 얼마예요?

An expression used to ask the price of something.

- 사과가 얼마예요?    How much are the apples?
- 수박이 얼마예요?    How much for a watermelon?
- 우유는 얼마예요?    How much is the price of milk?

★ Current denominations in Korean currency are ₩10, ₩50, ₩100, and ₩500 coins, and ₩1,000, ₩5,000, and ₩10,000. It is easiest to think of Korean money in terms of 10,000 as the basic unit.

★ When the number one is the first among many numbers, it is not usually pronounced. ₩10,000, for example, is said '만 원' instead of '일만 원'. ₩100,000 is read as '십만 원'.



**The difference between '이/가' and '은/는'**

'이/가' and '은/는' are both used as subject particles, but '은/는' functions to emphasize the topic and often is used in the making of comparisons.



**Complete the dialogues, based on the example.**

**Ex.**

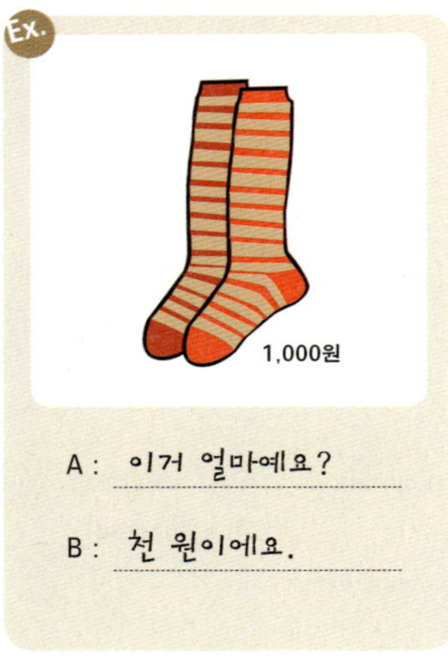



A : 이거 얼마예요?

B : 천 원이에요.

**1.**



A : ____________________

B : ____________________

**2.**



A : ____________________

B : ____________________

○ **얼마죠?**  How much is this/that/it?

A shortened form of "얼마지요?" that has the same meaning as "얼마예요?".

○ **만 원 주세요.**  Give me ten thousand won (for this).

Said in response to a question about price, used more frequently than "만 원이에요(₩10,000)."

○ **거스름돈 주세요.**  Give me the change.

Used when a customer wants to recieve the change after purchasing.



# Gomusin (Rubber Shoes) 고무신

Do you know what kind of shoes Koreans wear when they wear hanboks? In the old days they wore shoes made of leather or straw, but ones made of rubber quickly became popular because they are waterproof and practical. The first king to wear rubber shoes was Joseon's king Sunjong.

Rubber was once a precious material, so "black rubber shoes" were more common because they could be made from recycled rubber. You can't see them anymore. Eventually there came to be a lot of variety, with bleach used to make white shoes, shoes with flower designs for women, children's shoes, and other varieties. How would you like to try on a pair of rubber shoes? They're so comfortable you probably won't want to take them off.

# 저건 얼마예요?

## How much is that?

Track 009

: Dialogue

A 저건 얼마예요?
B 오천 원이에요.

A How much is that?
B It is 5,000 won.

Dialogue Tips

**오천 원이에요.**
**Five thousand won.**

An expression used to talk about price. You will also hear the formal form, "오천 원입니다."

---

**: Pronunciation Check**   오천 원이에요 [오처눠니에요]

**: Vocabulary & Expressions**

| | | | |
|---|---|---|---|
| 저거 that | 저건 that | 껌 gum | 이 two |
| 삼 three | 사 four | 육 six | 칠 seven |
| 팔 eight | 구 nine | | |

# N은/는 얼마예요?

An expression used to ask the price of something, in the context of comparing it to the price of something else you have just inquired about. When you ask about something for the first time, you use '이/가 얼마예요?' but both '은/는' and '이/가' may be omitted.



### Pronouncing '6'

Pronounced as [육] when the first syllable, [륙] when following a vowel or 'ㄹ', and as [뉵] when followed by 'ㅁ'. Note that when in front of '십' it is pronounced [심뉵].

- 저건 얼마예요? — How much is that?
- 사과가 얼마예요? — How much are the apples?
- 사과는 얼마예요? — The apples are how much?
- 수박이 얼마예요? — How much is a watermelon?
- A : 수박은 얼마예요? — A watermelon is how much?
  B : 만 원이에요. — Ten thousand won.

★ '저건' is often used as a reduced form of '저거는' in colloquial speech.

★ '이건' is a reduced form of '이거는' and '이게' is a reduced form of '이것이' in colloquial speech.

## Practice

**Complete the dialogues, based on the example.**

**Ex.**

A : (이거) __이거 얼마예요?__

B : (5,500원) __오천오백 원이에요.__

A : (저거) __저건 얼마예요?__

B : (10,000원) __만 원이에요.__

**1.** A : (저거) __________

B : (3,000원) __________

A : (이거) __________

B : (7,200원) __________

**2.** A : (물) __________

B : (1,000원) __________

A : (껌) __________

B : (500원) __________

**3.** A : (우유) __________

B : (1,500원) __________

A : (빵) __________

B : (500원) __________

- 비싸요. / 싸요.  (It's / That's) expensive./ inexpensive.

- 모두 얼마예요?  How much is the total price?

  Said when asking the total price of them after buying things

- 좀 깎아 주세요.  Cut some (off the price), please.

  An expression used when bartering that can be used in traditional markets or individually operated stores.

: Korean Insight

# Dojang (Personal Stamps) 도장

Have you ever used a personal stamp in Korea? These days, of course, the widespread use of credit cards to make purchases and the use of handwritten signatures instead of personal stamps for banking purposes they are less common than they used to be, but you still have to stamp documents with your personal dojang when finalizing a contract or for other important business.

That is why Koreans all have at least one. Companies and organizations also have stamps carved in their names. In days of old the king's stamp was considered so important that great effort was made to protect it during times of war. Most dojang are made of wood, but these days they are also made of plastic or the bones of animals. How about having a stamp carved in your name as a souvenir?

# 다섯 개 주세요.

Please give me five.

: Dialogue

**A** 사과 얼마예요?

**B** 한 개에 천 원이에요.

**A** 그럼 다섯 개 주세요.

A　How much for an apple?

B　They're a thousand won a piece.

A　Please give me five, then.

**Dialogue Tips**

**한 개에 천 원이에요.**
They're a thousand won a
piece.

Used to express the price
per unit of a given item.

: **Pronunciation** Check　다섯 개 [다섣깨]

: **Vocabulary &** Expressions

| | | | |
|---|---|---|---|
| 하나(한) one | 개 an item, a unit | 그럼 then, in that case | 다섯 five |
| 주다 to give | 둘(두) two | 셋(세) three | 넷(네) four |
| 씻다 to wash | | 명 unit for number of people | |
| 공책 notebook | | 권 unit for number of books or notebooks | |
| 주스 juice | | 잔 unit for number of cups or glasses | |
| 주세요 please give (me) | | 씻으세요 please wash | |

## V-(으)세요

An expression for respectfully telling someone to do something. If the verb stem is used with ends in a vowel, use '-세요' and if the stem ends with a consonant, use '-으세요'.

- 주세요.　　　　　　　　　　Please give (me).
- 씻으세요.　　　　　　　　　Please wash (it/that).

★　Note that the verb to eat, '먹다' becomes "드세요." and not "먹으세요."

★　Note that the verb to sleep, '자다' becomes "주무세요." and not "자세요."

## Counting Unit

Korean has diverse forms of what are called counters or counting units. When you count objects, use '개', when you count the number of people, use '명', when you count animals, use '마리', when you count bottles, use '병', and when you count books, use '권', and when you count cups or glasses, use '잔'.

- 사과 네 개 주세요.　　　　　Please give me four apples.
- 공책 두 권 주세요.　　　　　Please give me two books.
- 주스 한 병에 팔백 원이에요.　Juice is ₩800 a bottle.

★　When in front of counting units such as these, the numbers '하나, 둘, 셋, 넷' become '한, 두, 세, 네' respectively.

 **Complete the dialogues, based on the example.**

A : 사과 한 개에 얼마예요?

B : 천 원이에요.

A : 그럼 다섯 개 주세요. (5)

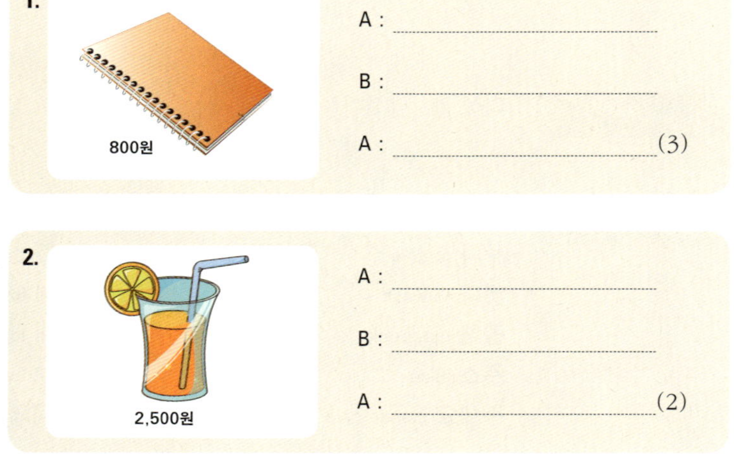


1.
A : ______________________

B : ______________________

A : ______________________ (3)

2.
A : ______________________

B : ______________________

A : ______________________ (2)

- **하나에 천 원이에요.**  They are ₩1,000 for one.

  The same meaning as "한 개에 천 원이에요." The counting unit has been omitted, but that is usually done only with '하나' and not other numbers.

- **세 개에 만 원이에요.**  They're 10,000 won for three.

- **다섯 개에 삼천 원이에요.**  Those are 3,000 won for five.



# Korean Dance Singers 한국의 댄스 가수

What Korean singers do you know? They say the "Korea wave" is overtaking Asia right now, and Korean dance singers are at the center of it all. The singer, "Rain" ("Bi") has enjoyed a lot of popularity and has performed in Asia and even the United States. The female dance singer, BoA, has excited the whole Japanese archipelago and become quite a star there. Rain, for his part, is all the more popular for his appearances on television dramas. There are other examples, as well, of Korean music artists earning popularity because of fine performances in films and dramas.

It would seem that the reason dance singers are so popular and enjoy such support from their many fans is that Koreans always have loved to make merriment.

These days there are a lot of young Korean students who want to sing for their careers. Why don't you take the chance to learn to sing a Korean song?

# 지금 몇 시예요?
## What time is it?

: **Dialogue**

A  실례합니다. 지금 몇 시예요?
B  세 시인데요.

A  Excuse me. What time is it?
B  It's 3 o'clock.



**실례합니다.** Excuse me.

An expression used when first approaching someone before speaking, or when interrupting someone.

**세 시인데요.** It's 3 o'clock.

'인데요' is a sentence ending, used with a noun. Used mostly in colloquial speech, frequently when you are going to continue with another sentence.

: **Pronunciation** Check

몇 시 [면씨]    여덟 시 [여덜씨]

: **Vocabulary &** Expressions

| | | | |
|---|---|---|---|
| 지금 now, right now | 몇 what, how | 시 the hour, o'clock | 분 minute |
| 여섯 six | 일곱 seven | 여덟 eight | 아홉 nine |
| 열 ten | 열하나/열한 eleven | 열둘/열두 twelve | 십오 fifteen |
| 이십 twenty | 이십오 twenty five | 삼십 thirty | 삼십오 thirty five |
| 사십 forty | 사십오 forty five | 오십 fifty | 오십오 fifty five |
| 실례합니다. Excuse me. | | | |

## 몇 N

Usually means "How many N," and so is used in relation to questions about number. When you ask the time, ask "몇 시예요?" When you ask how many there are of something, ask "몇 개예요?"

- 몇 시예요?  What time is it?
- 몇 개예요?  How many (of something) are there?
- 몇 명이에요?  How many people are there?

## Reading the Time : □시 □분이에요

Different types of numbers are used in front of ⋯⋯시 and ⋯⋯분.

| 1 | 2 | 3 | 4 | 5 | 6 | 7 | 8 | 9 | 10 | 11 | 12 | |
|---|---|---|---|---|---|---|---|---|----|----|----|---|
| 한 | 두 | 세 | 네 | 다섯 | 여섯 | 일곱 | 여덟 | 아홉 | 열 | 열한 | 열두 | + 시 |

| 1 | 2 | 3 | 4 | 5 | 10 | 15 | 20 | 25 |
|---|---|---|---|---|----|----|----|----|
| 일 | 이 | 삼 | 사 | 오 | 십 | 십오 | 이십 | 이십오 |

| 30 | 35 | 40 | 45 | 50 | 55 | |
|----|----|----|----|----|----|---|
| 삼십 | 삼십오 | 사십 | 사십오 | 오십 | 오십오 | + 분 |



**Complete the dialogues, based on the example.**

**Ex.**

A : 지금 몇 시예요?

B : 여섯 시인데요.

A : 고맙습니다.

**1.**

A : ⋯⋯⋯⋯⋯⋯⋯⋯⋯

B : ⋯⋯⋯⋯⋯⋯⋯⋯⋯

A : ⋯⋯⋯⋯⋯⋯⋯⋯⋯

**2.**

A : ⋯⋯⋯⋯⋯⋯⋯⋯⋯

B : ⋯⋯⋯⋯⋯⋯⋯⋯⋯

A : ⋯⋯⋯⋯⋯⋯⋯⋯⋯

○ **몇 시 몇 분이에요?**  What minute of what hour is it?

Used when you need to know the minute in question.

○ **30분/반, 55분/5분 전**  thirty/half, fifty five/five before

"Thirty" minutes can also be stated as "half." 1시 30분(한 시 삼십 분) is the same as '1시 반(한 시 반)' and 5시 30분(다섯 시 삼십 분) is the same as '다섯 시 반'. Also, 7시 55분(일곱 시 오십오 분) is the same as '여덟 시 오분 전', while 10시 50분(열 시 오십 분) can be stated as '열한 시 십분 전'.

: Korean Insight

# Gwisin (Korean Ghosts) 귀신

What scares you the most in this world? Many countries have famous ghosts, don't they? Korea has famous ghosts (gwisin),too. There are female ghosts who wear white hanboks and hair that extends over their faces.

There are messengers from the otherworld who come to claim the living. Then there are dokkaebi, who are not quite ghosts and are considered somewhat cute.

There are dokkaebi who carry "dokkaebi bats" and repeat mantras that make the wishes of people who have been good come true and play tricks on people who've been bad. Dokkaebi are said to become household objects during the daylight hours only to become dokkaebi again at night. Why not stay up tonight and see if any dokkaebi appear?

# 몇 시에 만날까요?
## What time should we meet?

**A** 몇 시에 만날까요?

**B** 내일 다섯 시에 만나요.

A  What time should we meet?
B  Let's meet tomorrow at five.

**몇 시에 만날까요?**
**What time should we meet?**

Used when making engagements. Used when you want to decide while respecting the views of the listener.

다섯 시 [다섣씨]

| | | |
|---|---|---|
| 영화 movie, film | 뭐 what | 사다 to buy |
| 만날까요? Shall we meet? | 후 later | |

# V-(으)ㄹ까요?

A question form used when you seek someone's views or desires while not strongly stating your own. It is similar to the English "Shall we ~?" When following a syllable that ends with a vowel this form is '-ㄹ까요?' and when following a consonant it is '-을까요?'.

**에**

A particle that follows the word '시간' to indicate the time at which an action takes place. Note that it is not omitted when following the time.

- A : 몇 시에 만날까요? — What time should we meet?
  B : 여섯 시에 만나요. — Let's meet at 6 o'clock
- A : 뭐 먹을까요? — What will we have?
  B : 빵 먹어요. — Let's have some bread.

★ When nothing further needs to be said, you can answer it with either "네" or "아니요".

- A : 영화 볼까요? — Shall we see a movie?
  B : 아니요. — No.
- A : 빵 먹을까요? — Should we have some bread?
  B : 네. — Yes.

★ When it is not a "Wh- question", "네, 좋아요, 그래요." is possible as the positive answer and "아니요." can be used as the negative answer.

- A : 바나나 살까요? — Shall we buy bananas?
- B : 아니요, 사과 사요. — No, let's buy apples.

: **Practice**  **Complete the dialogues, based on the example.**

**Ex.**

A : 몇 시에 (만나다)  → 몇 시에 만날까요?

B : (9시)  → 아홉 시에 만나요.

**1.** A : 뭐 (먹다)  → ___________________

B : (사과)  → ___________________

**2.** A : 몇 개 (사다) → ___________________

B : (2개)  → ___________________

**3.** A : 뭐 (마시다) → ___________________

B : (우유)  → ___________________

**4.** A : 어디 (가다) → ___________________

B : (도서관)  → ___________________

○ 언제 만날까요?  When should we meet?

A way to ask about determining a time to meet. In addition to actual time, '언제' can include the date and day of the week.

○ 내일 봐요.  See you tomorrow.

This means the same as "내일 만나요."

○ 삼십 분 후에 만나요.  See you in 30 minitues later.



# Korean Information Technology 한국의 IT

What country was your mobile phone made in? It seems many people know that Korea has a highly developed IT industry. "IT" stands for "information technology" and refers to technology relating to the processing, sending, and storage of information.

Korea has put a lot of IT products, like mobile phones, for example, on the global market. WiBro (Wireless Broadband Internet) technology produced in Korea was recently certified, increasing Korea's standing as an IT powerhouse. IT technology is used in medical equipment in addition to mobile phones and computers, and is contributing significantly to the development of medical equipment. It would appear that constant research and the drive for better products are what power the bright future of the Korean IT industry.

# 무슨 요일에 수영장에 가요?

## What day of the week do you go to the swimming pool?

: Dialogue

A  무슨 요일에 수영장에 가요?

B  토요일요.

A  What day of the week do you go to the swimming pool?
B  Saturday.

**Dialogue Tips**

**무슨 요일에 수영장에 가요?**  What day of the week do you go to the swimming pool?

Used to ask what day of the week an activity takes place on.


무슨 요일에 [무슨뇨이레]    토요일요 [토요이료]

| | | |
|---|---|---|
| 무슨 요일 what day of the week | 수영장 swimming pool | 토요일 Saturday |
| 월요일 Monday | 화요일 Tuesday | 수요일 Wednesday |
| 목요일 Thursday | 금요일 Friday | 일요일 Sunday |

## 무슨 N

Used to ask about the noun in question.

- 무슨 요일이에요?  What day of the week is it?
- 무슨 책이에요?  What book is it?

## N요

Used to give a simple answer to a question. Here "토요일요." is short for "토요일에 수영장에 가요."

- A : 몇 시예요?  What time is it?
  B : 9시요.  Nine o'clock.

- A : 무슨 요일에 가요?  What day of the week (do you) go?
  B : 일요일요.  Sunday.

★ "일요일에요." would be the correct form in this context, but in colloquial speech it is shortened to "일요일요."

**에**

This has many meanings.

① When used after words for time, date, or day of the week, it is similar to the English word "on".

Ex. 7시에, 화요일에

② When following a word for location and in combination with verbs like '가다' (to go) or '오다' (to come) it is similar to the English word "to".



Complete the dialogues, based on the example.

**Ex.**

(수영장에 가다 / 월요일)

A : 무슨 요일에 수영장에 가요?　　　B : 월요일에요. / 월요일요.

**1.** (친구를 만나다 / 수요일)

A : ________________

B : ________________

**2.** (영화를 보다 / 일요일)

A : ________________

B : ________________

- A : 오늘 무슨 요일이에요?  What day of the week is it today?

  B : 수요일이에요.  It's Wednesday.

- 수영장에 가요?/와요?  Will (you) go/come to the swimming pool?

  When the person being spoken to will be getting closer to the speaker say '와요'. When the person is going to become more distant in comparison to the speaker say '가요'.

# Misutgaru (Korean Beverages) 미숫가루

Korea has a diverse range of traditional drinks. Have you tried any? One among them, misutgaru, is made by steaming then roasting grains like beans, barley, glutinous rice, and non-glutinous rice or barley rice to make powder that is then used in a drink, with sugar added to meet one's taste.

In the old days misutgaru was a household drink in summer that was so common no house would be without it. They say that it was also used as an important form of emergency food for times of war. That's because it is plentiful in nutrients and is easy to digest, making it a possible alternative to a regular meal. These days it is a popular diet food among women. How about taking the time today to try misutgaru, which tastes good and is good for your health?

# 언제 한국에 왔어요?
## When did you come to Korea?

Track 014



: Dialogue

A 언제 한국에 왔어요?
B 일주일 전에 왔어요.

A When did you come to Korea?
B I came a week ago.

Dialogue Tips

**언제 왔어요?**
**When did you come?**
This can be asked of someone who is at the same location as the person asking the question.

: **Pronunciation** Check

일주일 [일쭈일]   왔어요 [와써요]

: **Vocabulary & Expressions**

| | | |
|---|---|---|
| 언제 when | 한국 Korea | 주일 a week |
| 일주일 one week | 전 before, ago | 달 a month |
| 한 달 one month | 영국 the United kingdom | |
| 삼 일(3일) three days / the third day of the month | | 호주 Australia |
| 어제 yesterday | 왔어요. (I) came. | |

# V-았/었어요

An informal past tense sentence ending.

❶ Is '-았어요' when with stems ending in the vowels 'ㅏ' and 'ㅗ'.

- 가다 → 갔어요
- 오다 → 오았어요 → 왔어요

❷ Becomes '-했어요' when used with verb stems in the '-하다' form.

- 공부하다 → 공부했어요

❸ Is '-었어요' when with stems not described in the following words.

- 먹다 → 먹었어요
- 배우다 → 배우었어요 → 배웠어요

★ To speak more formally, use '-습니다' with the stems described above to make '-았습니다', '-했습니다', and '-었습니다'.

  **Complete the dialogues, based on the example.**

Ex.

A : 김영 씨는 언제 한국에 왔어요?

B : 한 달 전에 왔어요.

1. A : 리사 씨는 언제 한국에 왔어요?

B : ________________________

2. A : 김영 씨는 언제 영국에 갔어요?

B : ________________________

2. A : 리사 씨는 언제 호주에 갔어요?

B : ________________________

- **오늘은 며칠이에요?**  What's today's date?

  This is how you ask the date.

- **오늘은 몇 월 며칠이에요?**  What is today's date?

- **유월 육 일이에요.**  It's the 6th of June.

  Be careful that it's not '육 월'.

- **시월 삼십일 일이에요.**  It's the 31th of October.

  Be careful that it's not '십 월'.

- **한 달 전에 왔어요.**  I came a month ago.



# Jukbuin (Bamboo Wife) 죽부인

Jukbuin means "Bamboo wife" or "Dutch wife" in Korean. Where did such a term come from? The name gives you a hint about what it is used for. Jukbuin is used in the summer months to help you sleep when it gets too hot. Used mainly in the homes of noble aristocrats, these devices were made by thinly cutting bamboo and tying the strands into the shape of a large pillow. A man would hug one to sleep with his arms and legs wrapped around it. It is empty inside so air flows through it, and the surface of the bamboo has a refreshingly cool feel to it, which helps reduce the heat when you're sleeping.

Jukbuin were probably the easiest of traditional Korean bamboo products to make. They were loved by men as much as their wives, because they provide physical and emotional comfort. Sometimes they would also take the place of the husband in noble households were positive feelings of emotion were rarely expressed towards women, because "Bamboo wives" could provide physical comfort for the womenfolk. Doesn't it have an interesting name? Sometime in the summer, when it's so hot you can't sleep, how about lying with your arms around a bamboo wife?

# 어디에서 봤어요?

Where did you see him/her?

A  가수를 봤어요.
B  어디에서 봤어요?
A  백화점에서요.

A  I saw a singer.
B  Where did you see him/her?
A  At a/the department store.

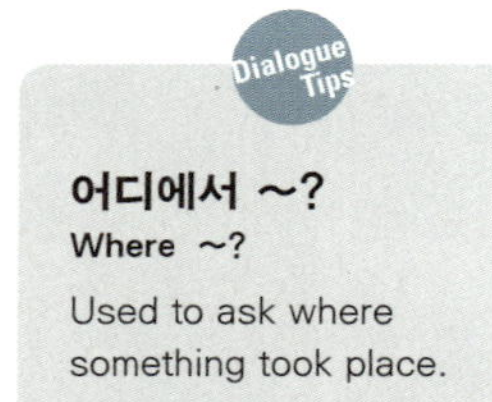


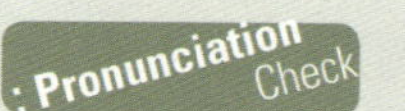
**Pronunciation Check**　　백화점 [배콰점]

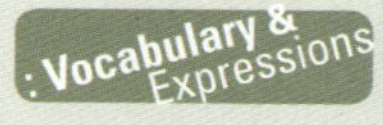
**Vocabulary & Expressions**

가수 singer, vocal performer　　읽다 to read　　밥 a meal, steamed rice
길 road, path, way　　커피숍 coffee shop　　커피 coffee

# N에서 V

A particle designating where action takes place. N is the noun for the place, V is the verb for what takes place there.

**에서**

A particle indicating where action transpired. It can mean "in," "at" or "from," but here is used to mean only the first two.

- 도서관에서 책을 읽었어요.  I read a book at the library.
- 식당에서 밥을 먹었어요.  I ate at a restaurant.
- 길에서 가수를 봤어요.  I saw a singer on the street ("in public").

- A : 어디에서 친구를 만났어요?  Where did you meet your friend?
  B : 커피숍에서 친구를 만났어요.  I met my friend in a coffee shop.

- A : 어디에서 책을 읽었어요?  Where did you read your book?
  B : 도서관에서요.  At a library.

## Practice

**Complete the dialouges, based on the example.**

**Ex.**

(가수를 보다 / 백화점)

A : 어디에서 가수를 봤어요?

B : 백화점에서요.

**1.** (책을 읽다 / 도서관)

A : ___________________________

B : ___________________________

**2.** (밥을 먹다 / 식당)

A : ___________________________

B : ___________________________

**3.** (커피를 마시다 / 커피숍)

A : ___________________________

B : ___________________________

**4.** (우산을 사다 / 백화점)

A : ___________________________

B : ___________________________

**5.** (친구를 만나다 / 학교)

A : ___________________________

B : ___________________________

- **여기에 사인해 주세요.**  Sign (your signature) here.

  Used when asking a famous individual for his or her autograph, when telling someone to authorize the use of his credit card, or when concluding a contract.

- **사인회가 있어요.**  There's an autograph-signing event.

  This means there is an event where an author or entertainment star gives out autographs.

# Hwaro (Charcoal Burner) 화로

It is hard to see hwaro, or charcoal burners these days, but in traditional Korean houses they were important instruments for enduring the cold of winter. Hwaro was used to preserve embers or cook food, and even to heat irons for ironing clothes.

Sometimes they were an easy way to heat potatoes or sweet potatoes for a quick snack in the middle of the night. You can imagine how important a role they played in everyday life.

Hwaro was made from a variety of materials. There were clay and china hwaro items which were made of earth. Others were made of metals like iron, bronze, and nickel. They were made into every shape imaginable. Some had beautiful designs carved into them.

The development of heating technology has led to their disappearance from our daily lives, but you can still see them used in restaurants to cook meat or boil jjigae. How about making a trip with your Korean friends to a restaurant that cooks with hwaro?

# 점심 먹었어요?

## Have you had lunch?

: Dialogue

A    점심 먹었어요?

B    아직 안 먹었어요.

A    그럼 같이 먹어요.

A    Have you had lunch?

B    I haven't eaten yet.

A    Then let's eat together.

**Dialogue Tips**

**점심 먹었어요?**

**Have you had lunch?**

Used usually after the hour when one eats lunch. It is used as a greeting expression.

Ex. 아침 먹었어요?

Have you had breakfast?

저녁 먹었어요?

Have you had dinner?

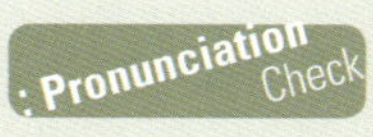
: Pronunciation Check

같이 [가치]

: Vocabulary & Expressions

| | | |
|---|---|---|
| 점심 lunch | 아직 not yet, still | 안 not (negates verbs) |
| 같이 together | 저녁 evening | 아침 morning |
| 식사 meal | | |

## 안 V

A short way to negate a verb.

- A : 저녁 먹었어요?　　Have you eaten dinner?
  B : 안 먹었어요.　　I haven't eaten (dinner).

- A : 집에 가요?　　Are you going home?
  B : 안 가요.　　I'm not going (home).

**그럼**

Say this when you recognize the validity of what someone has said and wish to present your own proposal or opinion in response.

## 아직

Means that an action hasn't taken places yet. It is frequently used with negative sentence forms. It implies there is the possibility the action may still happen.

- 밥을 아직 안 먹었어요.　　I haven't eaten yet.
- 집에 아직 안 갔어요?　　Haven't you gone home yet?
- A : 그 책 읽었어요?　　Did you read the book?
  B : 아니요, 아직 안 읽었어요.　　No, I didn't read yet.

 **Create the dialogues, based on the example.**

Ex.

(점심 / 먹다)

A : 점심 먹었어요?

B : 아직 안 먹었어요.

1.

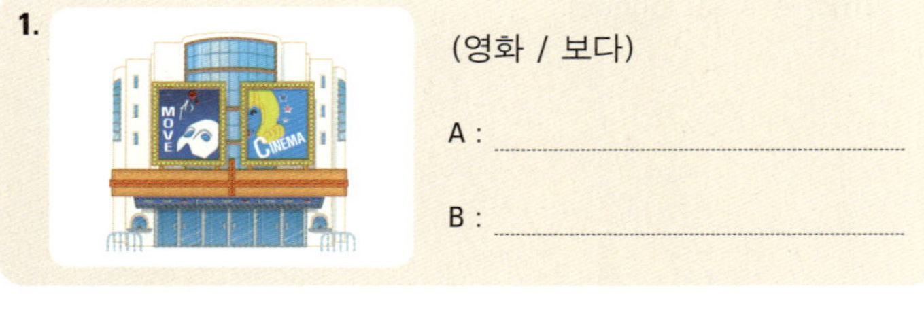

(영화 / 보다)

A : _______________

B : _______________

2.

(커피 / 마시다)

A : _______________

B : _______________

● **아침 드셨어요?**  Have you had breakfast?

Used mostly towards someone who is older than you, usually after the hour when one eats breakfast.

● **식사 하셨어요?**  Have you eaten?

Used mostly as a greeting to someone older, after regular mealtimes.

: Korean Insight

# Babsangbo (Meal Cloths) 밥상보

Have you ever heard of Korean "babsangbo?" A meal cloth is literally what it says it is, a pretty cloth for covering a meal that has been prepared on a table. In the past, if you didn't cover a meal as soon as it was ready, it was exposed to flies and dust, so meals were covered until the meal began.

Koreans have a tradition in which they do not begin to eat until the eldest in the house has begun to eat first. They say that if the eldest person present momentarily left the table, families would cover the meal with a meal cloth and wait. Babsangbo were often made from scraps of fabric left over from making new clothes. Nowadays they are found in picture frames or hung as wall decorations.

# 뭐 먹을까요?
## What should we eat?

A  뭐 먹을까요?
B  불고기 어때요?
A  좋아요.

A  What should we eat?
B  How about bulgogi?
A  Okay.

**Dialogue Tips**

**불고기 어때요?**
**How about bulgogi?**

An expression that indirectly suggests it would be good to have bulgogi.

**좋아요. Okay.**

It means you accept what someone has proposed.

: **Pronunciation** Check

좋아요 [조아요]

: **Vocabulary & Expressions**

| | | |
|---|---|---|
| 불고기 bulgogi | 쇼핑 shopping | 비빔밥 bibimbap |
| 어때요? how about ~? | 좋아요 good, okay, alright | |

# N이/가 어때요?

Used to make a proposition. The particle '이/가' may be omitted in colloquial speech.

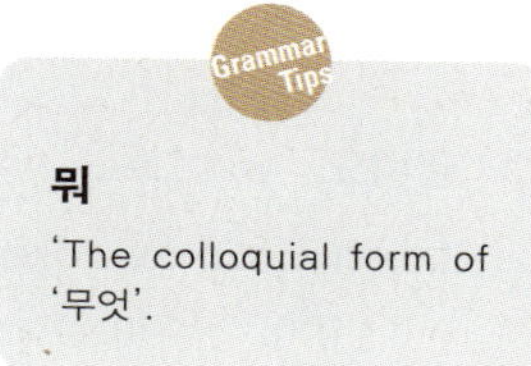

**뭐**

'The colloquial form of '무엇'.

- 불고기가 어때요?     How about bulgogi?
  불고기 어때요?     How about bulgogi?

- '킹콩'이 어때요?     How about "King Kong"?
  '킹콩' 어때요?     How about "King Kong"?

- 쇼핑 어때요?     How about (going) shopping?
- 비빔밥 어때요?     How about *bibimbap*?

**Practice**    Complete the dialogues, based on the example.

**Ex.**

(뭐 먹다 / 불고기)

A : 뭐 먹을까요?        B : 불고기 어때요?

**1.** (몇 시에 만나다 / 9시)

A : _______________________

B : _______________________

**2.** (어디 가다 / 백화점)

A : _______________________

B : _______________________

**3.** (뭐 마시다 / 커피)

A : _______________________

B : _______________________

**4.** (어디에서 공부하다 / 도서관)

A : _______________________

B : _______________________

- **그래요.** Alright. / Okay. / Fine.

  Similar to '좋아요', this expression means you accept someone's views.

- **글쎄요.** Well, I see.

  A colloquial expression used when you don't particularly agree with what someone has said, but aren't strongly opposed to it either.

- **그러지요.** Okay, let's.

  A more casual form for "그렇게 합시다." It would be best not to use this expression towards someone more advanced in age or of high social position.

: Korean
Insight

# Writing the Sound of Korean Laughter 한국의 웃음소리 표기

Have you ever chatted online or exchanged text messages with your Korean friends? Do you use a lot of emoticons? Koreans often transliterate the sound of laughter as '흐흐' or 'ㅋㅋ'. '흐흐' comes from Korean onomatopoeia like '하하', '호호', and '히히', while 'ㅋㅋ' is short for '큭큭' and '킥킥', the "sound" made when trying to keep yourself from laughing out loud. Then there's '프흐흐흐', short for sounds made when you're laughing hard, like '푸하하하' and '파하하하'. There are other ways to express laughter as well, such as "^^", "^_^", and "*^^*". You can use these emoticons when chatting online, in mobile phone text messages, or in emails to close friends. Try some of these "expressions."

# 불고기하고 냉면 주세요.
## Please give me bulgogi and naengmyeon.

Track 018

**: Dialogue**

A  뭐 드시겠어요?

B  불고기하고 냉면 주세요.

A  What will you eat/have?

B  Please give me bulgogi and naengmyeon.

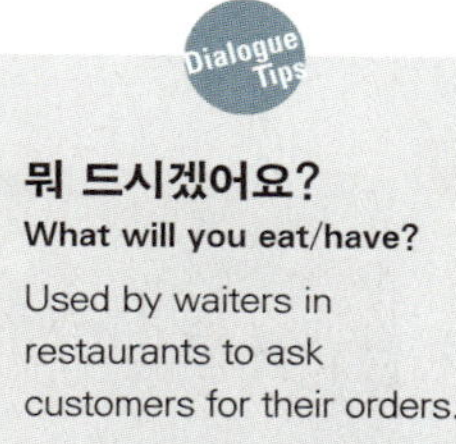

**Dialogue Tips**

**뭐 드시겠어요?**
**What will you eat/have?**

Used by waiters in restaurants to ask customers for their orders.



드시겠어요 [드시게써요]



드시다 to eat (honorific verb)　　　냉면 naengmyeon (lit. "cold noodles")
오늘 today　　　아이스크림 ice cream
바나나 banana　　　드시겠어요? Will you eat?

# N¹ 하고 N²

An expression used to indicate both N¹ and N². The positions of N¹ and N² are interchangeable.

- 빵하고 커피      bread and coffee
- 커피하고 빵      coffee and bread

★ A similar expression would be 'N¹와/과 N²'. If a word ends with a vowel use '와' and if it ends in a consonant use '과'. The order of N¹ and N² are interchangeable here as well.

- 빵과 커피      bread and coffee
- 커피와 빵      coffee and bread

> **Grammar Tips**
>
> **드시다**
> The honorific form for the verb '먹다'.

 **Make sentenses, based on the example.**

Ex.  

불고기하고 냉면 주세요.

1.  

______________________.

2.  

______________________.

- **주문하시겠습니까?**  Are you ready to order?

  **주문하시겠어요?**  Are you ready to order?

  **뭐 주문하시겠어요?**  What will you order?

  Phrases spoken when being asked for one's order in a restaurant.

- **주문하셨어요?**  Have you ordered?

  A way to ask if a customer has finished ordering.



## Jeju's Dokkaebi Road  제주 도깨비 도로

Have you been to Jeju island, one of Korea's best known vacation spots? Jeju has many famous places, but one among them is "Dokkaebi Road." It was given that name because it is full of surprises, just like dokkaebi. The typography on both sides gives the human eye the illusion that you are going uphill, when in fact the road goes downhill.

So if you place a bottle in the middle of the road, it rolls downhill while giving you the illusion that it is going up an incline. Many people tried this and they think it is interesting and mysterious. Thus, the short strip of road became a tourist destination. If you ever visit Jeju, make sure you stop by "Dokkaebi Road."

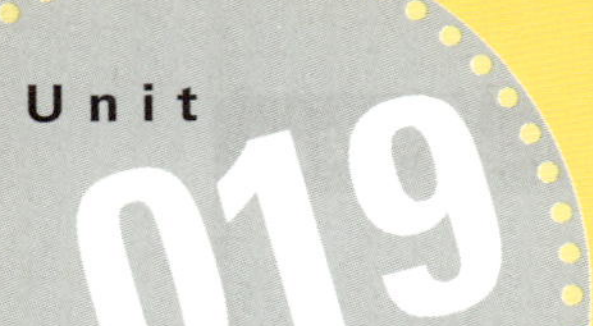

# 정말 맛있어요.

It's really delicious.

Track 019

**A** 맛이 어때요?

**B** 정말 맛있어요.

A　How's the taste?
B　It's really delicious.

**Dialogue Tips**

**정말 맛있어요.**
It's really delicious.

An expression used to say something is really delicious.

**어때요?**
Colloquial for "어떻습니까?"

**: Pronunciation Check**　　맛있어요 [마시써요]　　맛없어요 [마덥써요]

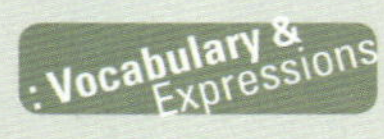

**: Vocabulary & Expressions**

맛 taste　　　　　　　정말 really　　　　　　맛있다 to be delicious
맛없다 to taste bad　　　옷 clothes

# N이/가 어때요?

A way to ask someone's thoughts about N.

- 이 책이 어때요?　　　　What do you think about this book?
- 한국이 어때요?　　　　How do you like Korea?
- 저 사람 어때요?　　　　How/what about that person?
- 이 영화 어때요?　　　　How is this movie?
- 이 옷 어때요?　　　　How are these clothes?
- A : 맛 어때요?　　　　How does it taste?
- B : 맛있어요.　　　　It's delicious.

**정말**

An adverb that works with an adjective to express degree. It is interchangeable with '아주'.

★　Here as well you can leave off the particle '이/가'. Here the expression as seen in "맛이 어때요?" is asking for an opinion, and so is different from "불고기 어때요?" in Unit 17.

 Practice　　**Make sentences, based on the example.**

**Ex.**

〈책〉

이 책이 어때요?

**1.**

〈빵〉

**2.**

〈아이스크림〉

- 맛이 괜찮아요?  Does it taste alright?

- 아주 맛있었어요.  It was very delicious.

- 별로예요.  Not really. Not so much/good.
  A colloquial expression that allows you to casually express your disagreement or disapproval.



# Sin Saimdang  신사임당

Do you know who is on the ₩5,000 Korean bill? That's Yi Yi, known also as Yulgok, a famous Confucian scholar. His mother, Sin Saimdang, is also well remembered today, as a fine poet and painter. There is a famous story about her that you should know. One day there was a party at a home nearby, and a woman there wearing a skirt she had borrowed got it stained with something.

The woman was distraught because she had no way to pay the owner for the skirt, but Sin Saimdang painted a bunch of grapes over the stain, allowing the woman to sell the skit for many times more than it was worth.

With that money she was able to buy several skirts and give the owner one even nicer than the one she had borrowed. Sin Saimdang was also an admirable mother who raised a famous Confucian scholar and a painter who had wit. A memorial has been built in her hometown to honor her and encourage young people to learn from her wisdom.

# 여기 물 좀 주세요.
## Please give me water.

**A** 김치가 정말 매워요.

**B** 여기 물 좀 주세요.

A　Kimchi is really hot.

B　Please give me water.

**여기 물 좀 주세요.**
**Please give me water.**

A polite expression you can use to ask for water. Put '주세요' at the end of what you are asking for when making your request.

**물 좀 주세요** [물좀주세요]

| | | | |
|---|---|---|---|
| 김치 kimchi | 좀 please | 맵다 to be spicy, hot | 쉽다 to be easy |
| 어렵다 to be hard, difficult | | 무겁다 to be heavy | 반찬 side dish |
| 매워요. It's hot. | | 어려워요. It's difficult. | 무거워요. It's heavy. |

# N이/가 A

A form used to explain the nature of N.

- 김치가 매워요.　　　　　Kimchi is hot.
- 불고기가 맛있어요.　　　 Bulgogi is delicious.
- 책이 재미없어요.　　　　 The book isn't interesting.
- 영화가 재미있었어요.　　 The movie was exciting.

★ The particle '을/를' never precedes an adjective.

**좀**
Similar to "please," and different from the '좀' that refers to quantity.

## ㅂ irregular conjugation

The infinitive of '맵다' is '맵다'. But when this verb is used with the informal sentence ending '-어요', the 'ㅂ' is replaced by the '우', and the '우+어요' becomes '-워요'.

- 맵다　　→　매워요
- 쉽다　　→　쉬워요
- 어렵다　→　어려워요
- 무겁다　→　무거워요

## Practice

**Make sentences, based on the example.**

여기 물 좀 주세요.

1.
________________________

2.
________________________

○ 여기요.(저기요.) / 주문 받으세요.  Excuse me. / Please take my order.

An expression frequently used to get the attention of a waiter and ask that your order be taken.

○ 여기 반찬 좀 더 주세요.  Please give us more of this side dish.

Use this expression to ask for a little more of the banchan that was placed at your table as part of what you ordered.



# DMB Mobile Phones  DMB 휴대폰

Do you like television dramas? Everyone who likes television dramas have had the experience of going home early to keep from missing the show time of her favorite drama. Now there's no reason to worry anymore, thanks to DMB (Digital Media Broadcasting) phones. Anyone who has a DMB-equipped mobile phone can watch a favorite television program while walking or while on the bus or subway.

These are phones that receive signals carrying television programming or other media and allow you to watch them on the phone's screen. There are two kinds of DMB; one transmits through satellites and the other transmits with terrestrial airwaves. It makes you wonder how far multimedia will develop in the future.

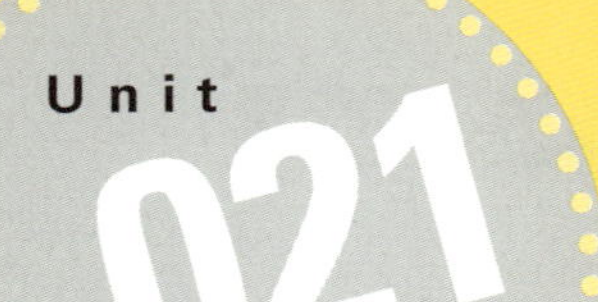



# 물 더 드릴까요?

Can I give you more water?

A  물 더 드릴까요?

B  아뇨, 괜찮아요.

A  Can I give you more water?
B  No, that's okay.

**Dialogue Tips**

**아뇨, 괜찮아요.**
No, that's okay.

An expression used to refuse an offer.
'괜찮아요' used to mean just "not bad", but these days it has come to be a clearly positive "good."

**Pronunciation Check**

괜찮아요 [괜차나요]

**Vocabulary & Expressions**

| | | |
|---|---|---|
| 더 more | 드리다 to give (honorific) | 아뇨 no |
| 괜찮다 to be okay, alright | 종업원 waiter/waitress | 손님 customer |
| 드릴까요? Shall I give ~? | 괜찮아요. That's alright. | |

# V-(으)ㄹ까요?

An expression used to propose something, similar to the English "Shall I ~?"



**아뇨.**
Colloquial for '아니요'.

- A : 뭐 드릴까요?  
  What can I give you?
  
  B : 냉면 주세요.  
  Give me naengmyeon, please.

- A : 물 더 드릴까요?  
  Would you like more water?
  
  B : 네, 더 주세요.  
  Yes, please give me some more.

★ If the stem ends in a vowel, use '-ㄹ까요?'. If it ends in a consonant, use '-을까요?'. It looks the same as '-(으)ㄹ까요?' in Unit 12 but has a different meaning.

## : Practice

**Complete the dialogues, based on the example.**

**Ex.**

종업원 : 어서 오세요. 뭐 드릴까요?

손님　: (불고기, 냉면) 불고기하고 냉면 주세요.

종업원 : (김치) 김치 더 드릴까요?

손님　: 네, 더 주세요. / 아뇨, 괜찮아요.

**1.**

종업원 : 어서 오세요. ___________________

손님　: (커피, 아이스크림) ___________________

종업원 : (커피) ___________________

손님　: 네, ___________ / 아뇨, ___________

**2.**

종업원 : 어서 오세요. ___________________

손님　: (우유, 빵) ___________________

종업원 : (물) ___________________

손님　: 네, ___________ / 아뇨, ___________

- 물 좀 더 갖다 주세요.   Please give me some more water.

- 더 필요한 거 있으세요?  Do you need anything else?

- 냅킨도 갖다 주세요.  Please bring us some napkins, too.
  A way to ask for napkins in addition to something else you've asked a waiter to bring to the table.

: Korean Insight

# Tteok and Tteoksal 떡과 떡살

Have you ever tried the Korean food known as "tteok"? In the past it was something enjoyed only on festive occasions and not something you had just any day of the week. Rice was once a scarce commodity, and making tteok requires a lot of it. To make especially pretty looking tteok, people used something called a "tteoksal." It might be easiest to think of a tteoksal as a Korean cookie cutter.

In the old days the different occasions required tteoksals that left imprints in the tteok that were distinctly appropriate for the event. Tteoksals are made of wood and are pretty enough on their own to be used today as decorative ornaments.

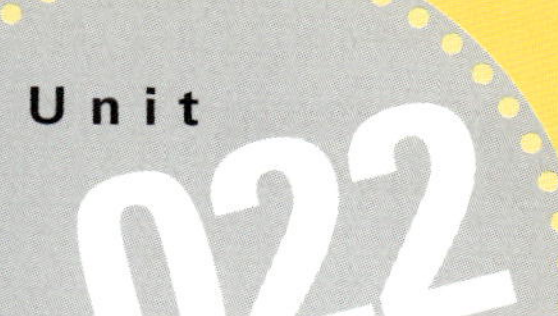

# 고추장은 빼 주세요.

## Please leave out the hot pepper paste.

Track 022

**A** 주문하시겠어요?

**B** 비빔밥 주세요. 고추장은 빼 주세요.

A  May I take your order?
B  Give me bibimbap. Please leave out the hot pepper paste.

**Dialogue Tips**

**주문하시겠어요?**
May I take your order?

Used by a waiter who has arrived ready to take your order.

---

**: Pronunciation** Check   비빔밥 [비빔빱]

---

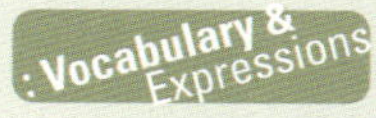
**: Vocabulary & Expressions**

| | | |
|---|---|---|
| 주문하다 to order | 고추장 hot pepper paste | 빼다 to leave out, remove |
| 김치찌개 kimchi jjigae | 후추 (black) pepper | 빼 주세요. Please leave out. |

---

# V-겠-

A formal expression used to reveal the speaker's intentions. It can be used only in the first person in declarative speech and only in the second person in interrogative speech.

- A : 주문하시겠어요?　　　　　Are you going to order?
  B : 네, 저는 냉면 먹겠어요.　　Yes, I'll have naengmyeon.

- A : 언제 오겠어요?　　　　　　When will you come?
  B : 내일 가겠어요.　　　　　　I'll go tomorrow.

**-시-**

This is attached to a verb stem to make an honorific expression. If the stem ends in a vowel use '-시-'. If it ends in a consonant, use '-으시-'. Since it "honors" the other person, you may not use it in reference to yourself.

Ex. 오**시**다, 읽**으시**다

---

# V-아/어 주다

Used to ask someone to do something for you or someone else. If the stem of the verb ends in a vowel 'ㅏ' or 'ㅗ', use '-아 주다'. If it is a '-하다' verb, this becomes '해 주다'. Any other verb, uses '-어 주다'.

- 후추는 빼 주세요.　　　Please leave out the (black) pepper.
- 지금 좀 와 주세요.　　　Please come now.
- 책 좀 읽어 주세요.　　　Please read this book.

★　When this is used as a sentence ending, as in '-아/어 주세요', you are making a request of someone.

**Practice**　Complete the sentences below using '-아/어 주다', based on the example.

**Ex.**

고추장을 (빼다) → 　고추장을 빼 주세요.

1. 책 좀 (읽다)　→　......................................................................

2. 지금 (주문하다)　→　......................................................................

3. 내일 (오다)　→　......................................................................

- **안 맵게 해 주세요.** Please don't make it hot.

  Say this if you are worried about your food being too spicy.

- **좀 맵게 해 주세요.** Please make it a little hotter than usual.

: Korean Insight

# Hangeul Internet Domains 한글 도메인

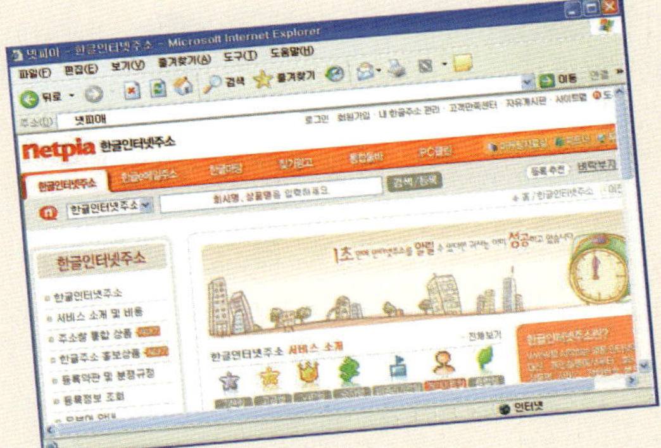

These days the first place you go to find information is the internet. The most important thing you need to know when surfing the internet is the domain of the webpage that has the information you're looking for, but most domains are in English, so if they get a little long they're hard to remember.

That's why in Korea there is something called "hangeul internet domains." Domains written in the Korean alphabet allow users to enter a website's address in Korean and be led to its more universal URL. It's a service that allows you to enter a word in Hangeul when you are unsure of a web page's English URL or when you only know one of the site's keywords. This really makes the internet friendlier for Koreans. You, too, will find it easy to find information this way while you're in Korea. It makes things especially easy when you are trying to find a news outlet or government department.

# 잘 먹겠습니다.
## Thank you for the meal.

Track
023

: Dialogue

A 많이 드세요.
B 잘 먹겠습니다.

A Enjoy your meal.
B Thank you for the meal.

**Dialogue Tips**

**잘 먹겠습니다.**
**Thank you for the meal.**

Said before you begin to eat a meal in a formal setting, for example when you are visiting a home or have been invited out to eat.

: **Pronunciation** Check

많이 [마니]    먹겠습니다 [먹껟씀니다]

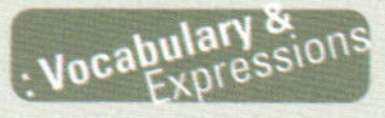
: **Vocabulary &** Expressions

많이 much, a lot              드세요. Please eat/enjoy.
잘 먹겠습니다. Thank you for the meal.

# Words Exchanged at Meals

**❶ 많이 드세요.**  Enjoy your meal.

Something said when you have invited a guest over, when you are paying for the meal, or to the person you are eating with if older than you.

**❷ 더 드세요.**  Please have more.

Used when that other person has all but finished, to suggest he have more.

**❸ 잘 먹었습니다./ 맛있게 먹었습니다.**  I ate well. / That was delicious.

Said when the meal is over, when leaving the table.

**잘**

'잘' most simply means all is fine or that something is done "well," but here it is used to mean you are "thankful" for the meal.

**Practice**  Pick the right expression to complete the sentences below.

| | | |
|---|---|---|
| 잘 먹겠습니다. | 뭐 드시겠어요? | 드세요. |

- Lisa and Kim Young enter a restaurant. Lisa will be buying a lunch today. -

리 사 : 오늘 점심은 제가 사겠어요.

종업원 : 어서 오세요. (1) ________________________

김 영 : 저는 냉면을 먹겠어요.

리 사 : 저는 비빔밥요. 냉면하고 비빔밥 주세요.

　　(Lunch arrives at the table⋯)

리 사 : 많이 (2) ________________________

김 영 : 네. (3) ________________________

- 배불러요. / 배가 불러요.  I'm full.

  Say this when someone has told you to "더 드세요." but you'd rather not because you're full.

- 배고파요. / 배가 고파요.  I'm hungry.



# Muui Island  무의도

Have you ever been to Incheon? As a port city, it is next to the sea and that makes for plenty of places to see. One among them is Muuido, or Muui Island, the set for the well-known Korean films "Stairways of Heaven" and "Silmido." Muuido gets its name from the fact that its shape looks like someone dancing with a military officer's clothes on. Islands nearby are called Daemuuido and Somuuido, for "large Muuido" and "small Muuido." Look a little farther and you'll see Silmido. Muuido is near Yeongjongdo (Yeongjong Island), where Incheon Internaitonal Airport is located.

You can get there by taking a ferry from the dock at Jamjindo, which you'll find if you go about 5 to 10 minutes from Yeongjong Bridge while following signs for Muuido. The natural scenery is beautiful and well preserved, and since you'll get to see the setting for Korean movies and television dramas it's well worth the trip.

# 저는 고기 안 먹어요.
## I don't eat meat.

A  왜 안 먹어요?

B  저는 고기 안 먹어요.

A  Why aren't you eating?
B  I don't eat meat.

저는 고기 안 먹어요.
I don't eat meat.

An expression for describing your preferences for food.

안 먹어요 [안머거요]

왜 why          고기 meat          닭고기 chicken

# 왜 V?

❶ Like the English word "why," this is used to inquire the reason for something.

- 왜 안 먹어요?      Why aren't you eating?
- 왜 집에 가요?      Why are you going home?
- 왜 책을 안 읽었어요?      Why didn't you read the book?

❷ The response is to answer with the reason.

- A : 왜 안 먹어요?      Why aren't you eating?
  B : 배불러요.      I'm full.

- A : 백화점에 왜 안 가요?      Why don't you go to the department store?
  B : 쇼핑을 싫어해요.      I don't like shopping.

**Grammar Tips**

**저는**

Used to highlight yourself or speak of yourself in contrast to someone else by comparison, use the particle '은/는' instead of '이/가'.

Ex. 저는 커피 안 마셔요.

---

**: Practice**    Complete the sentences below using '잘' or '안', based on the examples.

**Ex.**

고기를 좋아해요.

→ 고기를 잘 먹어요.

(먹다)

닭고기를 싫어해요.

→ 닭고기를 안 먹어요.

(먹다)

**1.**

아이스크림을 좋아해요.

→ 아이스크림을 ____________

(먹다)

**2.**

커피를 싫어해요.

→ 커피를 ____________

(마시다)

**3.**

쇼핑을 좋아해요.

→ 백화점에 ____________

(가다)

**4.**

책을 싫어해요.

→ 책을 ____________

(읽다)

- **고기를 잘 먹어요.** I enjoy meat.

- **고기를 안 먹어요.** I don't eat meat.

  This means you do not eat meat because you do not want to.

- **고기를 못 먹어요.** I can't eat meat.

  This means you might like meat, but for certain reasons are unable to have any, so are prevented from enjoying it.

: Korean Insight

# Hong Gildong 홍길동

Have you ever heard the name "Hong Gildong?" Everyone who has spent time living in Korea probably hears the name at least once. It's the name of a traditional fictional character, but it is also used like "John Doe," for example on sample forms you see in banks, airports, and public offices.

Hong Gildong is the name of the main character in the first Korean novel written in hangeul instead of literary Chinese, titled Hong Gildong Jeon. In the story he is portrayed as a Robin Hood type of figure who steals to help the poor. Every Korean knows the story, and that's how his name came to be the most common example of a name.

Recently, some scholars have begun to claim that the novel was based on a real character by that name. The township of Hwangnyong-myeon, in Jangseong-gu, South Jeolla province, claims it has restored the house Hong was born in and has turned the structure into a tourist attraction.

You, too, should take the time to visit his "birthplace" if you have an interest in someone who used mystical means to appear out of nowhere and vanish again as he punished those involved in corruption.

# 무슨 음식 좋아해요?

## What dishes do you like?

A  무슨 음식 좋아해요?

B  불고기요.

A  What dishes (food) do you like?

B  Bulgogi.

**Dialogue Tips**

**무슨 음식 좋아해요?**
**What dishes do you like?**

An expression used to ask what someone's tastes regarding food might be.

좋아해요 [조아해요]

| | | | |
|---|---|---|---|
| 음식 food | 좋아하다 to like | 색/색깔 color | 노란색 yellow |
| 파란색 blue | 다 all, everything | 과일 fruit | 빨간색 red |
| 무슨 음식 what food | 좋아해요. (I) like. | | |

# N을/를 좋아하다

This is used to express preferences, and you may omit the object particle '을/를' in colloquial speech.

- A : 무슨 음식을 좋아해요?  What food do you like?
  B : 불고기를 좋아해요.  I like bulgogi.

- A : 비빔밥 좋아해요?  Do you like bibimbap?
  B : 아뇨, 안 좋아해요.  No, I don't like bibimbap.

**-요**

'-요' is can be attached to the end of a word that is your short answer to a question. See Unit 13.

# 무슨 N

Though similar to the English word "what," it requires you mention a specific thing.

- A : 무슨 색깔 좋아해요?  What color do you like?
  B : 노란색하고 파란색을 좋아해요.  I like yellow and blue.

- A : 무슨 음식 먹었어요?  What food did you have?
  B : 비빔밥 먹었어요.  I had bibimbap.

★ Note that it may not be used in reference to a person or the character of something.

 Complete the dialogue, based on the example.

**Ex.**

A : 무슨 과일 좋아해요?

B : 포도 좋아해요.

**1.**

A : _______________________

B : 빨간색 좋아해요.

**2.**

A : _______________________

B : 비빔밥 좋아해요.

- **뭐 좋아해요?**  What do you like?

- **뭐 잘 먹어요?**  What do you enjoy (eating)?

- **다 잘 먹어요.**  I like everything.

  Use this expression when you mean to say you like all sorts of food and there's nothing you particularly try to avoid.



# The Korea Tourism Organization 한국관광공사

Where do you usually go for the information you need to travel within Korea? Have you heard of the Korea Tourism Organization? Its website (www.knto.or.kr) is full of diverse information about traveling in Korea. The Korea Tourism Organization is a government agency with the mission of growing the domestic tourism industry by developing "tourism technology" specific to Korea and creating attractive points of interest around the country that people want to visit over and over again. You can also call for information anywhere in the country by dialing 1330, 24 hours a day.

Its main office is right next to Cheonggyecheon, near where Cheonggyecheon begins in the Gwanghwamun area of downtown Seoul. It would be worth your time stopping by for maps and other information.

# 쇼핑 갈 거예요.

I'm going to go shopping

A 오늘 뭐 할 거예요?
B 쇼핑 갈 거예요.

A    What are you going to do today?
B    I'm going to go shopping.

**Dialogue Tips**

**오늘 뭐 할 거예요?**
**What are you going to do today?**

A way to ask inquire about someone's schedule.

**: Pronunciation** Check

할 거예요 [할꺼예요]    갈 거예요 [갈꺼예요]

**: Vocabulary & Expressions**

이번 this (time)          주말 weekend          쇼핑 가다 to go shopping
여행 가다 to go on a trip    등산 가다 to go hiking/mountain climbing
교회 가다 to go to church    할 거예요. I'm going to do.    갈 거예요. I'm going to go.

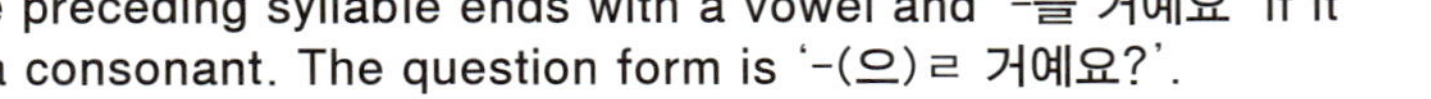

# V-(으)ㄹ 거예요

Used when asking, in the future tense, about what someone's future plans are. In this context first person is the subject and the subject when a question is the second person. Use '-ㄹ 거예요' when the preceding syllable ends with a vowel and '-을 거예요' if it ends in a consonant. The question form is '-(으)ㄹ 거예요?'.

**쇼핑 가다**

Here you can see that the object of the movement is "shopping." It's the same principle for '여행 가다' and '등산 가다'. If you want to emphasize the location the movement is directed at use '-에 가다'.

- 이번 주말에 여행 갈 거예요.    I'm going to go on a trip this weekend.

- A : 뭐 할 거예요?    What are you going to do?
  B : 쇼핑 갈 거예요.    I'm going to go shopping.

- A : 뭐 먹을 거예요?    What will you eat?
  B : 김밥 먹을 거예요.    I'm going to eat gimbap.

- A : 무슨 책 읽을 거예요?    What book are you going to read?
  B : 이 책 읽을 거예요.    I'm going to read this book.

 : Practice    **Make sentences, based on the example.**

**Ex.**

| Sun | MON | TUE | WED |
|---|---|---|---|
|  | 친구 / 만나다 | 오늘<br>공부하다 | 쇼핑 / 가다 |

오늘 뭐 해요? → 공부해요.

어제 뭐 했어요? → 친구 만났어요.

내일 뭐 할 거예요? → 쇼핑 갈 거예요.

**1.**

| Sun | MON | TUE | WED |
|---|---|---|---|
| 교회 / 가다 | 오늘<br>등산 / 가다 | 옷 / 사다 |  |

오늘 뭐 해요? → ___________.

어제 뭐 했어요 → ___________.

내일 뭐 할 거예요? → ___________.

**2.**

| THU | FRI | SAT | Sun |
|---|---|---|---|
|  | 친구 / 만나다 | 오늘<br>수영장 / 가다 | 수영장 / 가다 |

오늘 뭐 해요? → ___________.

어제 뭐 했어요 → ___________.

내일 뭐 할 거예요? → ___________.

- **오늘 뭐 해요?** What are you doing today?

  Used in reference to the current time or near future.

- **아직 잘 몰라요.** I don't know yet.

  Can be used when your day's schedule has yet to be determined.

- **오늘 약속 있어요.** I have an appointment today.

  This expression means that one has an appointment with someone today.



# Folk Remedies 민간요법

What do you do when you feel pain in your stomach? Do you take medicine? Do you go to a clinic or hospital? What did they do in the days when there were no hospitals and no pharmacies? In the old days mothers knew from experience various methods of reducing one's suffering.

Such remedies passed down through the generations are called mingan yobeop and Korea has many of them. For example, it is believed that thinly cutting green onion and placing it near your nose helps a head cold and that wrapping boiled red beans in cloth and putting it on the shoulder will help relieve shoulder pain. Other remedies include pricking a person's finger when he is having stomach pains related to indigestion, eating ginger to relieve nausea, or eating plums to fight diarrhea and stomachaches.

You might want to try a traditional Korean home remedy the next time you aren't feeling well.

# 청바지하고 모자 살 거예요.

I'm going to buy jeans and a hat.

Track
027

**A** 뭐 살 거예요?

**B** 청바지하고 모자 살 거예요.

A   What are you going to buy?
B   I'm going to buy jeans and a hat.

Dialogue Tips

**뭐 살 거예요?**
**What are you going to buy?**

An expression used when asking someone what he is going to purchase.

**: Pronunciation** Check   **살 거예요** [살꺼예요]

**: Vocabulary & Expressions**

| | | |
|---|---|---|
| 청바지 (blue) jeans | 모자 hat | 티셔츠 t-shirt |
| 원피스 one piece (dress) | 치마 skirt | 블라우스 blouse |
| 반바지 short pants | 바지 pants | 양복 suit |
| 넥타이 necktie | 스카프 scarf | 목도리 muffler |
| 바닐라 아이스크림 vanilla ice cream | 살 거예요. I'm going to buy. | |

# Terms for Korean Clothing

A considerable number of words for clothing are borrowed from foreign languages.

 티셔츠
t-shirt

 원피스
one piece (dress)

 치마
skirt

 블라우스
blouse

 반바지
short pants

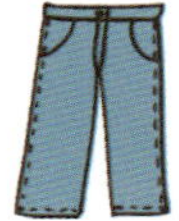 바지
pants

 양복
suit

 넥타이
necktie

 목도리
muffler

**Grammar Tips**

**Omission of '을/를'**

Words like '먹다', '사다', '만나다', and '보다' are proceeded by objects that reveal the "what" or "who" of the sentence. Object words should have object particles at the end of them, though they may be omitted in colloquial speech.

: **Practice**  Complete the dialogues, based on the example.

 Ex.

A : 오늘 뭐 할 거예요?

B : (쇼핑)  <u>쇼핑 갈 거예요.</u>

A : 뭐 살 거예요?

B : (블라우스, 스카프)  <u>블라우스하고 스카프 살 거예요.</u>


1.

A : 뭐 살 거예요?

B : (과일)  _______________________

A : 무슨 과일 살 거예요?

B : (사과, 바나나)  _______________________


2.

A : 뭐 먹을 거예요?

B : (아이스크림)  _______________________

A : 무슨 아이스크림 먹을 거예요?

B : (커피 아이스크림, 바닐라 아이스크림)  _______________________

- 도와 드릴까요?  May I help you?

- 그냥 구경만 할 거예요.  I'm just going to look.

  An expression used when you are in a store but don't intend to buy anything.

- 찾으시는 거 있으세요?  What are you looking for?

  Something a store employee might ask a customer.



# Dancing the Kkokjijeom 꼭짓점 댄스

The sight of Koreans cheering on the Korean national football team in front of Seoul City Hall during the 2002 World Cup came to be recognized around the world. During the 2006 World Cup as well, Koreans joined together to root for the home team.

One major difference between the mood in 2002 and 2006 was that people danced the "kkokjijeom." This special dance step became famous when a well-known actor performed it on television. It's especially fun to do in a group because it's easy to learn and everyone can share in a sense of oneness at the same time. See if you can find the steps to the kkokjijeom on the internet. It's easy enough that you'll be able to figure it out on your own.

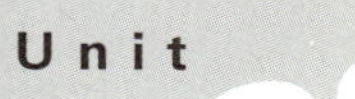

# 이거 입어 봐도 돼요?

May I try this on?

Track 028

A  이거 입어 봐도 돼요?
B  네, 이쪽에서 입어 보세요.

A  May I try this on?
B  Sure. You can try it on over there.

**Dialogue Tips**

**이거 입어 봐도 돼요?**
**May I try this on?**

An expression that tells a store employee that you would like to try on an article of clothing.

: Pronunciation Check

입어 [이버]    이쪽에서 [이쪼게서]

: Vocabulary & Expressions

| | | |
|---|---|---|
| 입다 to put on, wear | 신문 newspaper | 사무실 office |
| 담배 cigarette | 피우다 to smoke | 공원 park |
| 사진 photograph | 찍다 to take (a picture) | 이쪽 over here |
| 입어 보다 to try on | 쓰다 (모자를) to wear (a hat, eyewear) | |
| 입어 봐도 돼요? May I try (this) on? | | 입어 보세요. Try it on. |

: Grammar Focus

## V-아/어 보세요

An expression used when you want to tell someone to try doing something. If the stem of the verb for the action being tried ends in the vowels 'ㅏ' or 'ㅗ', attach it to the ending '-아 보세요'. If the verb being tried is a '하다' verb, the '하' of '하다' verbs becomes '해' to form '-해 보세요'. Attach all other verbs to '-어 보세요'.

- 와 보세요. — Please come (and see).
- 해 보세요. — Please try.
- 마셔 보세요. — Please try (drink).

> Grammar Tips
>
> **으 irregular conjugation**
>
> When conjugated in an informal sentence, '쓰다' and '크다' become '써요' and '커요' instead of '쓰+어요' and '크+어요'.
>
> Ex. 모자를 써요.
>
> 옷이 커요.

## V-아/어도 돼요?

An expression used to ask for permission or consent. Add '-아도 돼요?' if the verb stem ends in 'ㅏ' or 'ㅗ', '-해도 돼요?' if the verb you are using with this form is a '하다' verb, and '-어도 돼요?' with all other verbs.

- 지금 가도 돼요? — May I go now?
- A : 이 커피 마셔도 돼요? — Can I drink this coffee?
  B : 아뇨, 안 돼요. — No, you cannot.
- A : 수영해도 돼요? — Can I swim?
  B : 네, 수영해도 돼요. — Yes, you can swim.

★ The informal form of '되다' is '돼요', the formal form of '되다' is '됩니다'.

: Practice **Complete the dialogues, based on the example.**

Ex.

방 / 신문 / 읽다

A : 방에서 신문 읽어도 돼요?

B : 네, 읽어도 돼요.

1.

사무실 / 담배 / 피우다

A : ______________________

B : 아뇨, ______________________

2.

공원 / 사진 / 찍다

A : ______________________

B : 네, ______________________

- 입어 볼 수 있어요?  May I try (it, this) on?

  Another way to ask the same thing is "입어봐도 돼요?"

- 돼요. / 안 돼요.  Yes, you can. / No, you can not.

  These are ways to answer "-아/어도 돼요?", a question asking for permission or understanding. When you want to give consent say "돼요." When you don't want to give consent, say "안 돼요."

: Korean Insight

# Fortune  운수(운)

Have you ever heard of "un" or "unsu?" Both refer to the fate and opportunity you cannot control through your own strength. Koreans often say a particular day is an '운수 좋은 날' ("lucky day") or '운수 나쁜 날' ("unlucky day"). These days "un" is more frequently used for "fortune" than "unsu," so you might also hear Koreans say '운 좋은 날' more often.

When you buy something in Korea but want to return it, you will want to avoid the early morning hours and wait until afternoon. That is because if you return a purchase before a store owner has even begun to sell his wares, he might think a day of bad luck, '운이 나쁜 날', has begun.

On days of great importance, such as a wedding day or moving day, people usually chose days that will be '운 좋은 날', lucky days.

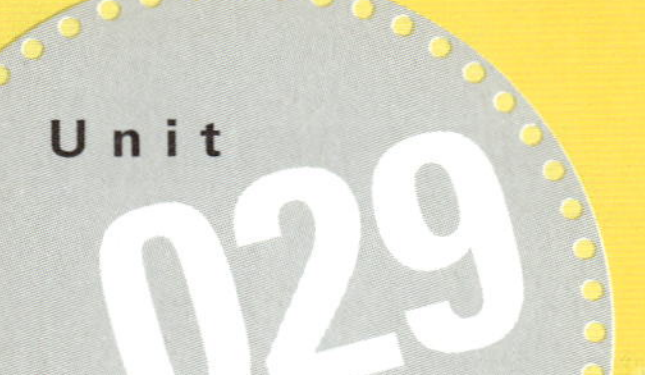

# 더 큰 거 있어요?

Do you have anything bigger?

**: Dialogue**

A 더 큰 거 있어요?

B 지금은 없는데요.

A Do you have anything bigger?

B Not right now.

**Dialogue Tips**

**더 큰 거 있어요?**

**Do you have anything bigger?**

When clothing you have tried on is too small or too tight, this is an expression you may use to ask for a larger size.

**: Pronunciation** Check

있어요 [이써요]    지금은 [지그믄]    없는데요 [엄는데요]

**: Vocabulary & Expressions**

| | | |
|---|---|---|
| 크다 to be big | 큰 big | 작다 to be small |
| 작은 small | 신발 shoe(s) | 노래 song |
| 숙제 homework | 두껍다 to be thick, heavy | 두꺼운 thick, heavy |
| 얇다 to be thin | 얇은 thin | 싸다 to be cheap |
| 싼 cheap | 큰 거 something big | 작은 거 something small |
| 두꺼운 거 something thick | 얇은 거 something thin, light | 싼 거 something cheap |

# A-(으)ㄴ데요

A sentence ending used frequently in colloquial situations. It is used together with adjectives that proceed it. When the adjective stem ends in a vowel, it is '-ㄴ데요' and when the stem ends in a consonant, it is '-은데요'. However, when it used with the verbs '있다' and '없다', it becomes '-는데요'. You hear this sentence ending in situations where there has been continued dialogue.

**'것' / '거'**

In this context, '것' is the object that is being referred to in the conversation. '거' is a spoken form of '것'.

이것 → 이거

저것 → 저거

큰 것 → 큰 거

작은 것 → 작은 거

- 옷이 좀 큰데요.　　　　　These (those) clothes are rather big.
- 신발이 작은데요.　　　　These shoes are small.
- 지금 없는데요.　　　　　We don't have any right now.
- 여기 있는데요.　　　　　Here it is.
- 김치가 좀 매운데요.　　　This kimchi's a little hot.
- 노래가 좋은데요.　　　　The song is good.
- 숙제가 어려운데요.　　　The homework is difficult.

★ Here '좀' is short for '조금', and so expresses degree or amount.

★ The conjugated form of '맵다' and 'A-(으)ㄴ데요' is '매운데요'. See the section on conjugating "irregular ㅂ verbs" in Unit 20.

 **Make sentences using the expression '-(으)ㄴ데요', based on the example .**

**EX.**

옷이 좀 비싸다.　→　__옷이 좀 비싼데요.__　　더 싼 거 있어요?

1. 모자가 좀 작다.　→　________________________　더 큰 거 있어요?

2. 신발이 좀 크다.　→　________________________　더 작은 거 있어요?

3. 바지가 좀 두껍다.　→　______________________　더 얇은 거 있어요?

4. 치마가 좀 얇다.　→　________________________　더 두꺼운 거 있어요?

● **더 큰 건 없어요?** Don't you have anything larger?

Say this when you have been shown an item by an employee but wonder if there is something larger. You can also ask "더 큰 거 있어요?"

● **더 싼 건 없어요?** Don't you have anything less expensive?

You're in a store and have just been shown a product by an employee. Use this question if you want to ask for something less expensive. You can also ask, "더 싼 거 있어요?"

: Korean Insight

# Hidden Treasures 숨겨진 명소

Gyeongbok Palace and Insa-dong are famous tourist destinations in downtown Seoul. Most of you reading this book have been to each place at least once.

There are other, less-known places to be enjoyed in Seoul beyond the usual tourist spots. One type of place that provides a different type of experience is the city's markets. You'll find fresh fish at the Noryangjin Fish Market and fresh fruit and vegetables at the Garak-dong Agricultural Products Market. If you visit either one of those markets in the early hours of the morning, you'll feel empowered by the sight of people working so hard. Another market that must be seen is Dongdaemun Market, where the action never stops. Many neighborhoods have their own, small-scale markets as well. There you'll find the kind of human touch you don't usually encounter in clean and organized supermarkets. Visit one when you get the chance.

# 이게 마음에 들어요.

I like this one.

Track
030

: Dialogue

A 어느 게 좋아요?
B 이게 마음에 들어요.

A Which one do you like?
B I like this one.

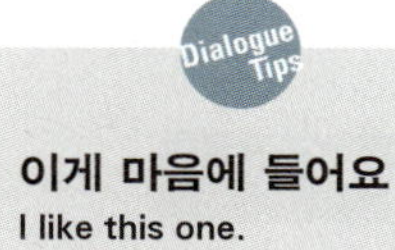

Dialogue Tips

**이게 마음에 들어요**
**I like this one.**

An expression for when you have been shopping and find what you want.

: Pronunciation Check

들어요 [드러요]

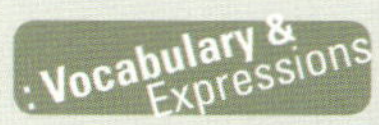
: Vocabulary & Expressions

어느 which  이게 this one  마음 mind
(마음에) 들다 to be satisfied  사탕 candy  마음에 들어요. I like.

# N이/가 좋다

Means the same as '좋아하다'. The subject may be the first person in declarative sentences, but in inquisitive sentences it is possible to use the second person.

- 저는 한국이 좋아요.　　　　I like Korea.
- 저는 한국을 좋아해요.　　　I like Korea.

- A : 이게 좋아요?　　　　You like this one?
- B : 아뇨, 싫어요.　　　　No, I don't like it.

★ '좋아하다' is a transitive verb, while '좋다' is an adjective that requires a different particle. Use '을/를' with '좋아하다' and '이/가' with '좋다'. The opposite of '좋다' is '싫다' and the opposite of '좋아하다' is '싫어하다'.

★ When using '좋다', the subject cannot be the third person.

**어느**

Use this word when you are asking about someone's choice of one among many. It must be followed by a noun.

Ex.

어느 학교 which school

어느 교실 which classroom

어느 집 which house

어느 것 which one/thing



**Complete the following sentences using '좋아요' or '좋아해요', based on the example.**

**Ex.**

저는 사과가 　좋아요　.

저는 사과를 　좋아해요.

**1.**

저는 냉면이 ______________

**2.**

저는 포도가 ______________

**2.**

저는 사탕을 ______________

**4.**

저는 리사를 ______________

○ **이건 어때요?**  How about this one?

Used when suggesting something.

○ **이건 어떠세요?**  How do you like this one?

Means the same as "이건 어때요?" but a more formal expression.

○ **마음에 드는 게 없어요.**  There's nothing I like (among these).

An expression used when there's nothing you're particularly interested in.

○ **이게 딱 좋아요.**  This is perfect.

A very colloquial expression for when you really like something.



# Han Seokbong and His Mother  한석봉과 어머니

Have you ever heard of Han Seokbong? Han lived from 1543 to 1605. He was a famous calligrapher, and there's a famous story about him and his mother. When he was young and still learning how to do traditional calligraphy he got so good that one day he thought he had nothing left to learn. Later he was visiting his mother in his hometown, and she came up with an idea for making modest again.

She proposed that in the dark of night she cut tteok and he write calligraphy to see who was better at their respective activity. When their little experiment was over, his mother had cut perfect slices of tteok, but it was impossible to make out what he had written. Han returned to Seoul and studied diligently, and that is how he became famous for his craft. Today the story is told to young people so that they might know the value of humility, because you never learn all there is to know.

# 이게 더 예쁘죠?

## This one's prettier, isn't it?

: Dialogue

**A** 이게 더 예쁘죠?

**B** 네, 그래요.

A   This one's prettier, isn't it?
B   Yes, it is.

**이게 더 예쁘죠?**
**This one's prettier, isn't it?**

Say this when there is something you like more in comparison to something else and want affirmation from the other person.

---

예쁘죠 [예쁘조]

예쁘다 to be pretty     따뜻하다 to be warm     비싸다 to be expensive

운동화 sneakers, running shoes     구두 shoes (more formal than sneakers)

편하다 to be comfortable     형 elder brother     연필 pencil

볼펜 ball point pen     예쁘죠? (Is it) pretty?

## N¹이/가 N²보다 더 A

An expression for making comparisons. N² is the object being compared. This pattern can be used to compare two items, not three or more.



**이게**

A colloquial contraction for '이것이'. Similarly, '저것이' and '그것이' are also shortened to '저게' and '그게' respectively.

- 이게 저거보다 더 비싸요.  This is more expensive than that.
- 오늘이 어제보다 더 따뜻해요.  It's warmer today than it was yesterday
- 운동화가 구두보다 더 편해요.  Sneakers are more comfortable than dress shoes.
- A : 누가 더 커요?  Who is bigger (taller)?
  B : 동생이 형보다 더 커요  The younger brother is bigger than the older one.

★ N²보다 N¹이/가 더 A
You may also change the order of what is being compared.

- 저거보다 이게 더 비싸요.  More so than that, this is expensive.
- 어제보다 오늘이 더 따뜻해요.  It's hot today, more than it was yesterday.
- 구두보다 운동화가 더 편해요.  Sneakers are more comfortable than formal shoes.

★ 'N²보다' or '더' can be omitted, but not both.

- A : 어느 게 더 비싸요?  Which one is more expensive?
  B : 이게 저거보다 더 비싸요.  This is more expensive than that.
  = 이게 저거보다 비싸요.  This is more expensive than that.
  = 이게 더 비싸요.  This is more expensive.

 **Make sentences, based on the example.**

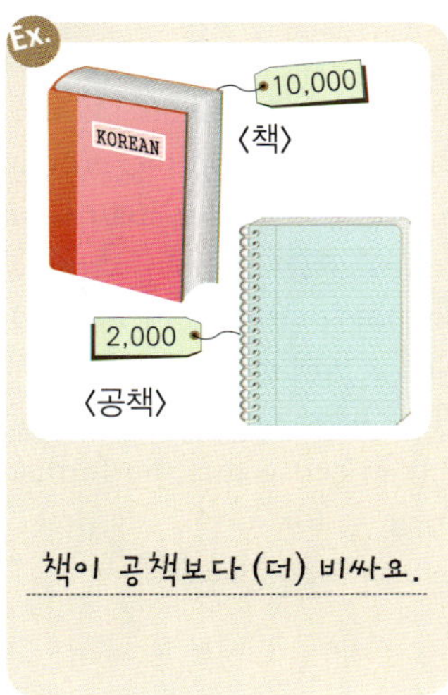


책이 공책보다 (더) 비싸요.

**1.**

(크다)

**2.**

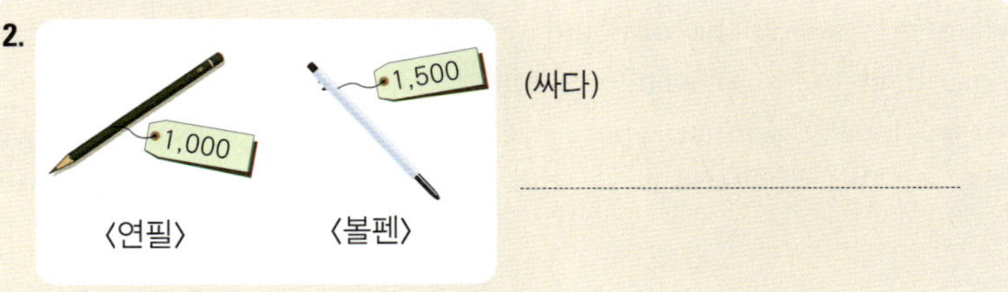


(싸다)

- **어느 게 더 좋아요?**  Which one is better? (Which one do you prefer?)

- **뭐가 더 좋아요?**  What is (would be) better?

  A way to ask someone's preference. Note that Koreans often ask what would be translated into English as "What is better?" or "What is nicer (for you)?" when in English you would say "What do you like?"

- **저게 좀 더 싸죠?**  That's more inexpensive, isn't it?

  When you see an item at something of a distance and it is likely less expensive, ask this of someone in the know for confirmation.

- **누가 더 커요?**  Who is bigger?

  An expression for asking for comparison of people.



# Traditional Weddings 전통 혼례

Most Koreans get married in wedding dresses and tuxedos. However, lately traditional ceremonies are making something of a comeback. The bride and groom wear a special kind of hanbok for traditional weddings instead of the style of hanbok you see worn on other occasions.

In traditional times the groom would go to the bride's house and have the ceremony there. The bride would then be carried on a palanquin while the groom rode on a horse to the home of the groom's family. These days, with people living in apartment complexes, holding wedding ceremonies in homes is just impossible. Nowadays people wanting to have traditional ceremonies can go to sites designed especially for the purpose. In the old days the bride and groom would see each other's faces for the first time during the ceremony, when they would be directed to bow to each other and pledge to live happily ever after, but these days the significance of traditional ceremonies is to be found only in sense that the format is traditionally Korean. There are places that stage traditional weddings just for tourists, so take time out this weekend to go and see what a proper Korean wedding used to look like.

# 이거로 할게요.

I'll have this one.



## : Dialogue

A  이거로 할게요.

B  더 필요한 거 없으세요?

A  I'll have this one.

B  Do you need anything else?

Dialogue Tips

**더 필요한 거 없으세요?**
**Do you need anything else? Will that be all?**

Something frequently said by a store employee to a customer who is done shopping and about to pay.

**: Pronunciation** Check     할게요 [할께요]     필요한 거 [피료한거]     없으세요 [업쓰세요]

**: Vocabulary & Expressions**

| | | |
|---|---|---|
| 로 by using this/that | 필요하다 to need | 거 thing |
| 갈비탕 galbitang | 만들다 to make | 꽃 flower(s) |
| 저 that | 자리 seat | 삼계탕 samgyetang |
| 백합 lily | 장미 rose | 장갑 gloves |
| 다른 another, different | 쪽 side | 고르다 to choose |
| 할게요. I'll (V). | 없으세요? Do you not have? | |

# V-(으)ㄹ게요

This expresses the intention of the speaker, by the speaker, usually in the process of making a commitment or decision. This pattern has no interrogative form.

- 지금 갈게요.　　　　　　　I'm going now. I'll go now.
- 공부 열심히 할게요.　　　　I'll study hard.

- A : 뭐 먹을 거예요?　　　　What will you have to eat?
- B : 저는 갈비탕 먹을게요.　　I'll have galbitang.

★　If the verb stem ends in a vowel, use '-ㄹ게요', if ends in a consonant, use '-을게요', except if that consonant is a 'ㄹ', this 'ㄹ' is dropped and use '-ㄹ게요'.

- 가다 → 갈게요　　　먹다 → 먹을게요　　　만들다 → 만들게요

# N(으)로 할게요

A way to say you've made your choice in a situation requiring you to choose among many.

- 꽃으로 할게요.　　　　　　I'll go with flowers.
- 저 자리로 할게요.　　　　　I'll take that place (seat).
- 삼계탕으로 할게요.　　　　　I'll have samgyetang.

**Grammar Tips**

**N(으)로**

If the last letter in N ends in a vowel use '-로', if it ends in a consonant use '-으로', unless it ends in a 'ㄹ', for which you should use '-로'.

 Make sentences, based on the example.

Ex.

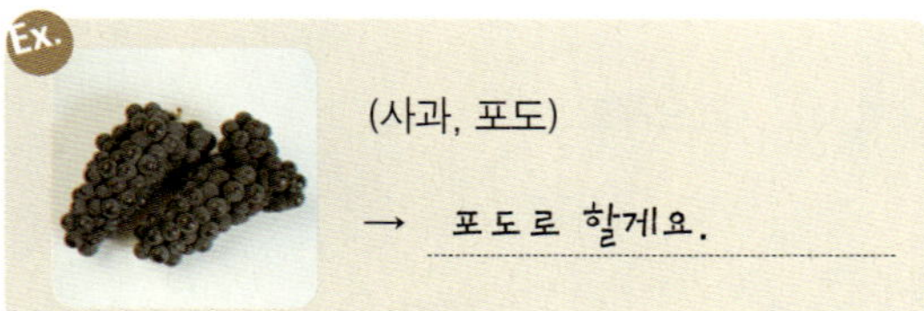

(사과, 포도)

→　포도로 할게요.

1.

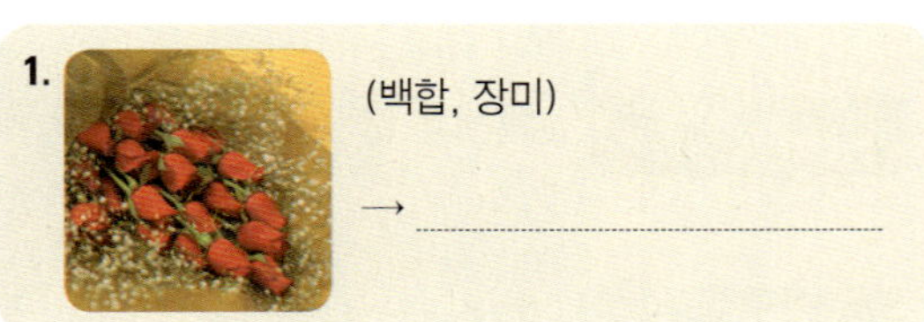

(백합, 장미)

→ ______________________

2.

(비빔밥, 삼계탕)

→ ______________________

3.

(장갑, 모자)

→ ______________________

- **다른 쪽도 보셨어요?**  Have you looked in another area (another part of the same store)?

  A way for an employee to suggest you shop more within the same store.

- **다 고르셨어요?**  Have you chosen all (you need to)?

  A way to ask someone if he is ready to stop shopping, having found everything he needs to.

# Tofu (Bean Curd) 두부

Tofu is probably one of the most widely consumed food ingredients in Korea. No one is sure when Koreans first began eating bean curd, but it makes its first appearance historical records from the late Goryeo period. Meat was something of a commodity at times, and so tofu was a good source of protein. Recently it has been popular among women as a diet food.

Bean curd goes into a lot of Korean dishes. The most typical, of course, would be sundubu, which often gets served as a jjigae, as in sundubu jjigae, and is a popular lunch menu amongst professionals. Why not have some for lunch today? Sundubu jjigae is rich in nutrients and inexpensive.

# 정말 싸네요.
## That's really cheap.

: Dialogue

A 모두 얼마죠?
B 이만 원만 주세요.
A 정말 싸네요.

A How much is this all together?
B That'll be 20,000 won.
A That's really cheap.

**Dialogue Tips**

**모두 얼마죠?**
**How much is this all together?**

Say this when you have chosen various items and are ready to pay for them all at once.

**정말 싸네요.**
**That's really cheap.**

A exclamatory sentence that expresses surprise at the fact something is not as expensive as assumed.

: Pronunciation Check

이만 원만 [이마뭔만]    얼마죠 [얼마조]

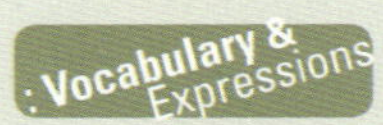
: Vocabulary & Expressions

모두 all, everyone, everything
문제 problem, question, issue
싸게 inexpensively (adverb)

만 only
비 rain

명동 Myeongdong (area of Seoul)
깎다 to cut off, to reduce (price)

## 얼마죠?

Usually 'N(이)지요?' is used to ask for agreement, but if the N is replaced with an interrogative word the phrase becomes a regular interrogative phrase and not one seeking confirmation.

**N-(이)죠?**

This is the contracted form of 'N-(이)지요?'. The '죠' is to be pronounced [조].

- 얼마죠? — How much is this?
- 지금 몇 시죠? — What time is it (right now)?
- 여기가 어디죠? — Where is this? ("Where are we?")

★ This phrase is only to be found in the interrogative form, so when you answer you should use 'N이에요' or 'N 예요'.

- A : 얼마죠? — How much?
  B : 이만 원이에요. — It's (that'll be) twenty thousand won.

- A : 지금 몇 시죠? — What time is it?
  B : 열두 시예요. — It's twelve o'clock.

- A : 여기가 어디죠? — Where are we?
  B : 명동이에요. — This is Myeongdong.

## A/V-네요

An expression for being exclamatory.

- 정말 맛있네요. — This is (that was) really delicious.
- 문제가 어렵네요. — That's a difficult problem.
- 비가 오네요. — It's raining.

 **Make the questions, based on the example.**

A : 여기가 어디죠?    (여기, 어디)

B : 운동장이에요.

1. A : _____________________    (지금, 몇 시)

   B : 9시예요.

2. A : _____________________    (오늘, 무슨 요일)

   B : 수요일이에요.

3. A : _____________________    (저 사람, 누구)

   B : 리사 켈리예요.

◯ **할인 되죠?**  Can this be discounted?

◯ **좀 싸게 해 주세요.**  Please make it cheap.

Phrases you can use when bargaining over price.

◯ **거스름돈 받으세요.**  Here's your change. ("Take your change.")

◯ **세일이에요.**  Discount.



# Makgeolli (Raw Rice Wine) 막걸리

Know which among Korea's alcoholic drinks has the longest history? That would be none other than makgeoll, the fermented wine that looks white like milk and contains, among other things, barley and flour. It is very inexpensive, and they say farmers would drink a little while working to regain strength.

Since it is made from grains, it simultaneously quenches thirst and helps fight a sense of hunger. It is widely enjoyed by Koreans today, especially among the "common" people and young university students. Typical anju (side dishes for alcoholic drinks) are pajeon and kimchi. The next time it rains, why not go with your friends to a Korean-style drinking establishment and have makgeolli and pajeon?

# 카드 돼요?

Do you take credit cards?

## : Dialogue

A 카드 돼요?

B 네, 됩니다.

A  Do you take credit cards?
B  Yes, we do.

**Dialogue Tips**

**카드 돼요?**
**Do you take credit cards?**
**Is a credit card okay?**

You need to ask this in a store when you want to pay for something that is under 5,000 won or it looks like the store only accepts cash.

**됩니다** [됨니다/뛈니다]

| | | |
|---|---|---|
| 카드 a card, credit card | 되다 to be okay, alright | 토마토 tomato |
| 소설책 a novel | 오렌지 orange | 콜라 cola |
| 팥빙수 patbingsu | 영수증 receipt | |
| 돼요? Do you take?, Is this/that acceptable? | | 됩니다. That is acceptable. |

# N이/가 돼요?

An expression for asking whether N is possible or permitted, often used in situations where you are shopping, making an order, or making an appointment. In colloquial conversation the particle '이/가' often gets omitted.

**Is it '돼요?' or '되요?'**

Even native speakers of Korean get confused about this. The informal sentence ending for '되다' is '되+어요', which is to be written '돼요'. The formal form is '되+ㅂ니다', or '됩니다'. '되요' is incorrect.

- A : 토마토 주스 돼요?　　Can I have tomato juice?
  B : 네, 돼요.　　Yes, you can.

- A : 이번 수요일 돼요?　　Is Wednesday alright?
  B : 아뇨, 안 돼요.　　No, it isn't.

# V-는데요

A sentence ending that must be attached to a verb. It is common in colloquial speech and usually used in a context in which it is expected the conversation is an ongoing one.

- A : 어디 가요?　　Where are you going?
  B : 학교에 가는데요.　　I'm going to school.

- A : 무슨 책 읽어요?　　What book are you reading?
  B : 소설책 읽는데요.　　I'm reading a novel.



**Complete the dialogues, based on the example.**

Ex.

A : 오렌지 주스 돼요?

B : 네, 되는데요.

〈오렌지 주스〉

1.

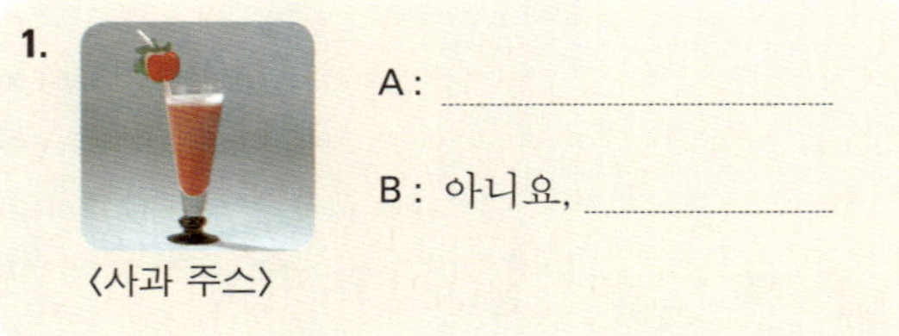

A : ________________

B : 아니요, ________________

〈사과 주스〉

2.

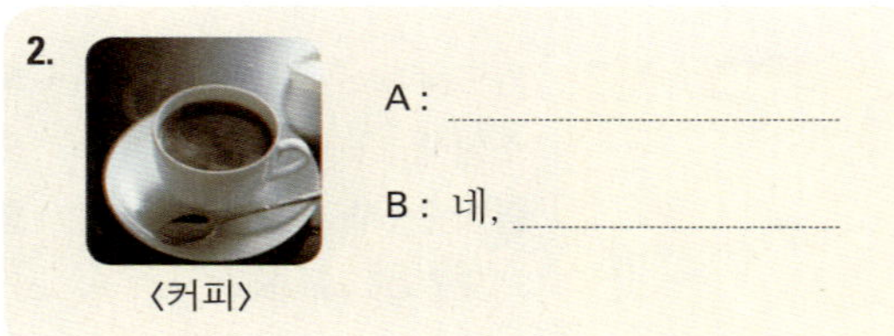

A : ________________

B : 네, ________________

〈커피〉

- **여기 서명해 주세요.**  Please sign here.

  You'll hear this when asked to sign a receipt after using a credit card.

- **계산서 주세요.**  Please give me the bill.

  An expression for requesting a statement of expenditures, for the purpose of settling the bill.

- **영수증 주세요.**  Please give me a/the receipt.

  An expression for asking for a receipt.

: Korean Insight

# Deungmok (Back Bathing) 등목

Korea has four distinct seasons: spring, summer, fall, and winter. Summers are very hot and rain is frequent, so it's humid, too. Temperatures can reach as high as 35 degrees Celsius. These days you'll find air conditioning wherever you go, but in the days when there weren't electric fans and air conditioners, people had a variety of ways to fight back the heat.

One of those was deungmok, or "back bathing," which was a way to cool off when you didn't have time for a shower. It involved taking off your shirt but leaving your pants on while extending your rear end into the air while someone else pours cold water on your back.

Every Korean has seen someone "bathing his back" at least once. It was a quick and easy way to cool off, but sadly it was never something women could do.

# 모자 사러 가요.

Let's go to buy a hat.

**A** 다 됐어요?

**B** 아뇨. 이제 모자 사러 가요.

A   Are you all done/ready?
B   No. Next let's go to buy a hat.

**다 됐어요?**
**Are you all ready?**
A way to ask someone if he has finished what he is doing.



---

**Pronunciation** Check

됐어요 [돼써요/뒈써요]

---

**Vocabulary & Expressions**

| | | |
|---|---|---|
| 편지 a letter | 부치다 to send (letter, package) | 우체국 post office |
| 빌리다 to borrow, lend | 테니스 tennis | 치다 to hit |
| 테니스를 치다 to play tennis | 컴퓨터 computer | 쇼핑센터 shopping center |
| 공항 airport | 극장 theater | 차 tea |
| 다 됐어요? Are you ready/done?, Is everything complete? | | |

# V-(으)러 가다

This lets someone know what the object of movement is. Also possible are 'V-(으)러 오다' and 'V-(으)러 다니다'.

- 친구 만나러 가요.　　　　　　I'm going to meet a friend.
- 편지 부치러 우체국에 가요.　　I'm going to the post office to mail a letter.
- 책 빌리러 도서관에 가요.　　　I'm going to the library to borrow a book.
- 김 선생님 좀 만나러 왔어요.　I'm going to meet Mrs. Kim for a while.

- A : 어디 가요?　　　　　　　Where are you going?
  B : 테니스 치러 가요.　　　　I'm going to play tennis.

★ If the final letter in a verb stem ends in a vowel or 'ㄹ', use '-러'. If it ends in a consonant, use '-으러'.

- 배우다 → 배우러　　먹다 → 먹으러　　만들다 → 만들러

**'이제' and '지금'**

'지금' refers only to the exact present, while '이제' expresses discontinuance in relation to the past. Someone who has not been exercising very much but intends to from now on needs to say "이제 운동을 열심히 할 거예요." instead of "지금 운동을 열심히 할 거예요." The latter of these means something close to "I'm going to exercise hard from now on."

 **Complete the dialogues, based on the example.**

**Ex.**
A : 어디 가요?
B : **과일 사러 슈퍼에 가요.**
　　(과일, 사다, 슈퍼)

**1.** A : 어디 가요?
B : ______________________
　　(컴퓨터, 사다, 쇼핑센터)

**2.** A : 어디 가요?
B : ______________________
　　(친구, 만나다, 공항)

**3.** A : 어디 가요?
B : ______________________
　　(영화, 보다, 극장)

**4.** A : 어디 가요?
B : ______________________
　　(차, 마시다, 커피숍)

**5.** A : 어디 가요?
B : ______________________
　　(책, 빌리다, 도서관)

- **아직요.**  (Not) yet.

- **아직 안 끝났어요.**  I'm not done yet.

  Ways to tell someone you are yet to be finished with something.

- **다 돼 가요.**  I'm almost done.

  A way to say you're near completion of the task at hand.



# Simcheong Jeon 심청전

Simcheong Jeon is a story of an exceedingly dutiful daughter and is a classic Korean story. One day a girl named Simcheong is sacrificed to the ocean in order to make her blind father see. Once in the water, however, the Dragon King (who resides in the ocean) is so touched by her filial piety that he allows her to return to the realm of humans, and it is there she marries the king and lives happily ever after while caring for her father.

Filial piety towards one's parents was long considered one of the greatest of virtues in Korea. Today a woman who is especially respectful of her parents and takes particularly good care of them is sometimes called a "Simcheong, the filial daughter." The Korean belief in the virtue of having a "filial heart" has led the public to feel the need to show respect for all elders, and not just one's own parents. That is why you see people vacating seats for elderly people on busses and subways. There are also seats designated as being reserved for the elderly. While you're in Korea, how about giving your seat to elderly passengers while taking public transportation?

# 택시로 가요.

I go by taxi.

A 집에 뭐 타고 가요?

B 택시로 가요.

A What do you ride to get home?

B I go by taxi.

**택시로 가요.**

**I go by taxi.**

These are expressions used to describe the means of transportation.

집에 [지베]    택시 [택씨]

| | | |
|---|---|---|
| 타다 to ride | 택시 taxi | 타고 가다 to go by riding |
| 지하철 subway | 버스 bus | 배 boat, ship |
| 오토바이 motorcycle | 비행기 airplane | 어떻게 how |
| KTX(Korea Train Express) Korea's high speed rail | | 타고 가요. I go by riding on. |

# N(으)로 가다

There are many meanings to '(으)로', but in this sentence form you reveal what method of transportation you are using by attaching it to the end of the noun for that form of transport. You can use '오다' instead of '가다'.

- 택시로 가요.　　　　　　　I take a taxi.
- 버스로 왔어요.　　　　　　I came by bus.
- 배로 갈 거예요.　　　　　　I'll go by boat.

- A : 뭐 타고 갈까요?　　　　What should we/I take to get there?
- B : 지하철로 가요.　　　　　Let's go by subway.

★　If the last syllable of the noun ends in a vowel use '로'. If it ends in a consonant use '으로', unless it ends in the consonant 'ㄹ', in which case also use '로'.

- 택시로　　　　　　　　　　by taxi
- 지하철로　　　　　　　　　by subway

**N을/를 타고 가다/오다**

An expression similar to 'N(으)로 가다/오다'. It requires the use of the object particle '을/를', though that may be deleted in colloquial speech. Movement is expressed by saying '타고 가다/오다' instead of just '타다'.

: Practice　　**Make the sentences, based on the example.**

Ex. 
A : 뭐 타고 왔어요?
B : 택시로 왔어요.

1. 
A : 뭐 타고 가요?
B : ________________

2. 
A : 뭐 타고 왔어요?
B : ________________

3. 
A : 뭐 타고 갔어요?
B : ________________

◦ **집에 어떻게 가요?**  How do you get home?

An expression for asking how someone goes home.

◦ **걸어 왔어요. / 걸어서 왔어요.**  I walked to get here.

A expression saying you walked instead of using another means of transportation.

◦ **KTX 타고 갈 거예요.**  I'll go by KTX.

An expression that tells someone you intend to travel by Korea's high speed rail system, KTX.

: Korean Insight

# Straw Craftwork 짚 공예

Jip is the Korean word for the straw that comes from jipuragi, which is what remains from rice plants after the rice has been harvested. Koreans have grown and eaten rice for centuries, and they have used the remaining jipuragi for a variety of purposes. They make rope from it, called saekki.

With the rope they then make bags called mangtaegi and wicker baskets called sokuri. Straw mats called meongseok, similar to what you might call a carpet, are also produced from the same kind of straw, as are shoes made of jip. Jipsin were never worn by the rich, but they were once popular among the common people. They say that back before Korea had active commercial economy, people made whatever they needed at home. It's hard to see things made of jip in everyday life these days, but you should be able to see common articles made from the material if you go to the Korean Folk Village or rural areas.

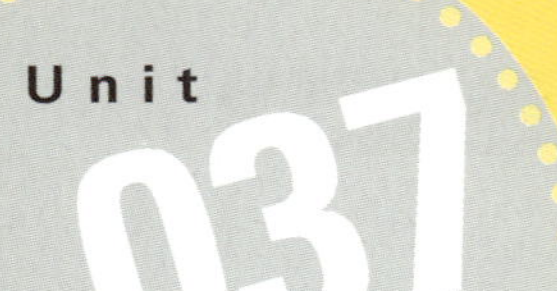

# 집에 혼자 갈 수 있어요?

Can you go home by yourself?

Track 037

**: Dialogue**

A  집에 혼자 갈 수 있어요?
B  네, 여기서 가까워요.

A  Can you go home by yourself?
B  Yes, it's close to here.

**Dialogue Tips**

**집에 혼자 갈 수 있어요?**
**Can you go home by yourself?**

Something you might ask of someone if you worry he might not be knowledgable about where he is and how to use public transportation.

**: Pronunciation** Check  집에 [지베]  갈 수 있어요 [갈쑤이써요]

**: Vocabulary & Expressions**

| | | |
|---|---|---|
| 혼자 alone, by oneself | 에서 from | 가깝다 to be close |
| 오후 afternoon | 같이 together | 못 not, can't |
| 살다 to live | 멀다 to be far | 가까워요. It's close. |
| 멀어요. It's far. | | |

# V-(으)ㄹ 수 있어요?

An expression for discussing ability or possibilities. It will work only with verbs. It can be used as both an interrogative and declarative sentence ending.

- 지금 올 수 있어요?  Can you come now?
- 오후에 만날 수 있어요?  Can we meet in the afternoon?
- 혼자 갈 수 있어요?  Can you go by yourself?
- A : 병원에 혼자 갈 수 있어요?  Can you go to a hospital by yourself?

  B : 아뇨, 혼자 못 가요.  No, I can't go to a hospital by myself.

★ If the final syllable in a given verb stem ends in a vowel, use '-ㄹ 수'. If it ends in a consonant, use '-을 수'. However, if the consonant is a 'ㄹ', omit that 'ㄹ' and use '-ㄹ 수'.

- 가다  →  갈 수 있어요
- 먹다  →  먹을 수 있어요
- 살다  →  살 수 있어요

**여기서 / 여기에서**

The '에서' of '여기에서' means "from". '여기서' is an abbreviated form of '여기에서'. You can shorten '에서' to '서' when it is attached to a pronoun but not a noun.

Ex. 학교에서 (O)
　　학교서 (X)



**Complete the dialouges below, based on the example.**

Ex.
A : 저는 오늘 학교에 안 가요.

B : (같이 밥 먹다) 같이 밥 먹을 수 있어요?

1. A : 저는 내일 미국에 가요.

   B : (오늘 만나다) __________

2. A : 오늘은 시간이 없어요.

   B : (내일 오다) __________

3. A : 삼계탕 먹으러 가요.

   B : (삼계탕 먹다) __________

4. A : 오후에 공항에 갈 거예요.

   B : (혼자 가다) __________

5. A : 신문을 샀어요.

   B : (읽다) __________

- 여기서 금방이에요. It's just a little ways.

  Say this if something is nearby and thus easy to get to.

- 여기서 멀어요. It's far from here.

  This means it's far.

- A : 여기서 걸어갈 수 있어요? Can I walk from here?

  B : 아뇨, 걸어갈 수 없어요. No, you can't walk (there).

  Question A is a way to ask if something is close. B is an answer to question A, meaning the destination is not close.



# Madangnori 마당놀이

Have you ever heard "ganggangsullae?" Ganggangsullae is one of Korea's traditional madangnori, which, in turn has many meanings but in the larger sense it refers to a folk activity done in a yard or public space. Koreans farmed for generations, and Korea had a lot of madangnori, which gave people time with the community during lulls in the agricultural season. All these activities, therefore, are related to parts of the year when there is not much work to be done on the farm. During the first month of the lunar year, people traditionally did kite flying (yeonnalligi), gossaumnori, and soemeoridaegi. During the fifth month of the year they would do ssireum (wrestling) and geunettwigi (swing riding). During Chuseok they would play juldarigi (tug-of-war) gamassaumnori (palanquin fighting), and jangchigi (field hockey). There are a total of eleven such madangnori.

These days it is hard to see any of them firsthand, but you can try some of them at the Korean Folk Village or, during Seollal or Chuseok, at palaces in major cities. If you're in Korea, why not go to a palace on a traditional Korean holiday and try a madangnori ?

# 여기에서 얼마나 걸려요?

How long does it take from here?

Track 038

**A** 여기에서 얼마나 걸려요?

**B** 걸어서 10분쯤 걸려요.

A  How long does it take from here?
B  It's a ten minute walk.

**Dialogue Tips**

**여기에서 얼마나 걸려요?** How long does it take from here?

An expression for asking how much time it take to get to a destination.

**: Pronunciation** Check

걸어서 [거러서]

**: Vocabulary & Expressions**

얼마나 how much time, how long (distance)

쯤 about, around　　　　　우리 we, our, us　　　　까지 to

켤레 a pair (of shoes)　　　경주 Gyeongju　　　　일본 Japan

걸려요 it take(s)　　　　　걸리다 to take (time)

# N이/가 걸려요

An expression for asking how much time it takes for something. The particle may be omitted in colloquial speech. It is usually used in the pattern 'A에서 B까지 N이/가 걸려요'.

**쯤**

Used to express an approximation, when you don't know the exact time or amount of what is being discussed.

- 우리 집에서 학교까지 한 시간이 걸려요.

  It takes an hour from our house to school.

- A : 여기서 얼마나 걸려요?  How long does it take from here?

  B : 삼십 분쯤 걸려요.  About thirty minutes.

★ When a 'ㄹ' is in the first position of a syllable you usually pronounce it by a quick touch your tongue to the roof of your mouth (for example in the word '우리'). However, when the last letter in one syllable is a 'ㄹ' and it leads directly to another 'ㄹ' in the first position of the next syllable, the first ㄹ is pronounced as if it is the last letter being pronounced (as in '물').

- 지하철로  by subway
- 구두 한 켤레  one pair of shoes



**Complete the dialouges, based on the example.**

**Ex.**

A : (집, 학교) 집에서 학교까지 얼마나 걸려요?

B : (1시간) 한 시간쯤 걸려요.

**1.** A : (집, 공항) ______________

B : (2시간) ______________

**2.** A : (집, 슈퍼) ______________

B : (30분) ______________

**3.** A : (집, 경주) ______________

B : (5시간) ______________

**4.** A : (여기, 저기) ______________

B : (25분) ______________

**5.** A : (한국, 일본) ______________

B : (1시간 30분) ______________

- 여기서 한참 걸려요. It takes a while from here.

- 여기서 오래 걸려요. It takes a long time from here.

  An expression for saying that a lot of time will be required to cover what is a significant distance.

- 여기서 얼마 안 걸려요. It doesn't take long from here.

  An expression for saying that going the distance in question will consume a lot of time.

- 학교까지 지하철로 30분 걸려요. It takes 30 minutes from school to the subway.

  An expression for also discussing the method of transportation.



# Pajeon 파전

A lot of people think that most Korean food is hot and spicy, like kimchi. However, there are plenty of Korean dishes that are not hot and are quite delicious. Pajeon is one among them. It is rich in nutrients and is made from producing dough from flour and adding green onion, onion, seafood, and other ingredients. It is a healthy dish because it provides carbohydrates, fat, vitamins, minerals, and protein all that the same time.

It is most often consumed as anju, dishes enjoyed with alcoholic beverages, and it considered a particularly appropriate match for makgeolli. There's an area of Busan called Dongnae that is especially famous for pajeon. Be sure to visit Dongnae to have some when you have the chance. Koreans especially like to have makgeolli and pajeon on rainy days. How about having a bowl of makgeolli and some pajeon with your Korean friends the next time it rains?

# 택시 어디서 타요?

Where should I catch a taxi?

Track
039

A 택시 어디서 타요?
B 여기서 타면 돼요.

A Where should I catch a taxi?
B You can take one from here.

**Dialogue Tips**

**여기서 타면 돼요.**
**You can take one here.**

An expression the used to tell someone he can take his method of transportation where he is currently, without having to go anywhere.


택시 [택씨]　　돼요 [돼요/뒈요]


내리다 to get off　　　정류장 (bus) stop　　　떠나다 to leave, depart
T-Money(티머니) T-Money (Korean transportation card)　　　지하철역 subway station

# V-(으)면 돼요

**An expression used to express that it is acceptable or sufficient for something to happen. It may be used with an adjective as well.**

- 지금 가면 돼요.   You can go now.
- 다음 정류장에서 내리면 돼요.   You may get off at the next stop.
- T-Money만 있으면 돼요.   All you need is T-Money.

★  T-Money is a type of electronic card used for paying for public transportation. They are sold in set amounts and then maybe "recharged" and have their value replenished.

★  If a verb's last syllable ends in a vowel use '-면'. If it ends in a consonant use '-으면'. The exception is when a verb ends with a 'ㄹ', in which case use '-면'.

- 내리다   →   내리면 돼요
- 읽다   →   읽으면 돼요
- 살다   →   살면 돼요

**: Practice**   **Complete the dialogues below, based on the example.**

**Ex.**

A : 언제 떠나요?

B : (지금 떠나다)  지금 떠나면 돼요.

---

**1.** A : 다 됐어요?

B : (물만 사다) __________

---

**2.** A : 우리 어디에서 만나요?

B : (극장 앞에서 만나다) __________

---

**3.** A : 이 책 어디까지 읽어요?

B : (5과까지 읽다) __________

---

**4.** A : 버스 어디서 타요?

B : (저기서 타다) __________

---

**5.** A : 내일 몇 시에 가요?

B : (3시에 가다) __________

- **버스 정류장이 어디예요?**  Where is the bus stop?

  An expression for asking where the bus stop is.

- **지하철역이 어디 있어요?**  Where is the subway station?

  An expression for finding where the subway station is.

- **택시 타는 곳이 어디예요?**  Where does one catch a taxi?

  An expression for asking where a taxi stop is.

- **여기서 타야 돼요.**  You must take it (from) here.

  An expression for saying that the desired form of transportation may not be boarded elsewhere.

: Korean Insight

# Ttakjichigi  딱지치기

Do you know how to do ttakjichi? This is a game children used to play in the street involving "ttakji," which are made by children using thick paper or sold in stores and made from printed cardboard.

Players decide by a round of "rock, paper, scissors." The person that wins gets to play first, and everyone else puts their ttakji on the ground for him to try to flip with his ttakji by throwing it at the ground with all his strength. If he succeeds in flipping a ttakji on the ground he claims it as his and he can continue to play. If he fails to flip someone else's ttakji, the order of play changes. There has always been a little variety according to region, so for example you may be required to displace an opponent's ttakji to outside a circle or get your ttakji to go underneath another one.

It has become harder to see children playing ttakjichigi these days, because children play computer games every chance they get, instead of playing outside. Nowadays it is gradually more of a pastime from the past, something that carries a lot of nostalgia with it for those who grew up before the digital era.

# 집에 들어가면 전화하세요.
## Call me when you get home.

Track
040

A  먼저 갈게요.
B  네. 집에 들어가면 전화하세요.

A  I'll be going now. ("I'm going (home) first.")
B  Okay. Call me when you get home.

Dialogue Tips

**먼저 갈게요.**
**I'll be going now.**

Something said by someone who is with a group of people but is leaving before everyone else, to those who are going to remain.

: **Pronunciation** Check

갈게요 [갈께요]　　집에 [지베]

: **Vocabulary &** Expressions

| | | |
|---|---|---|
| 먼저 first | 들어가다 to enter | 전화하다 to telephone |
| 배고프다 to be hungry | 날씨 weather | 좋다 to be good, nice, alright |
| 산 mountain | 비가 오다 to rain | |

# V¹–(으)면 V²

A conditional clause. Once the condition(s) of what precedes the clause are met, that which is described in the phrase that follows then becomes possible. Since the speaker is talking about a condition that has yet to be met, the phrase that follows is expressed in the future tense or with a sentence ending that implies the future. Adjectives may also be used with this pattern.

- 집에 들어가면 전화하세요.　　Call when you get (inside) home.
- 배고프면 빵 좀 드시겠어요?　　If you're hungry, will you have some bread?
- 날씨가 좋으면 산에 갈 거예요.　　If the weather is pleasant, I'm going to go to a mountain.
- 김치가 안 매우면 많이 먹을 수 있어요.　　I'm going to have a lot of kimchi if it isn't hot.
- 비가 오면 도서관에 안 갈 거예요.　　If it rains, I'm not going to go to the library.
- 시간 되면 같이 쇼핑 갈까요?　　If you are free, would you go shopping with me?

**· Practice**　　**Make sentences, based on the example.**

**Ex.**

날씨가 좋아요.

→ (산에 가다) 날씨가 좋으면 산에 갈 거예요.

**1.** 옷이 비싸요.

→ (안 사다) _______________

**2.** 영화가 재미있어요.

→ (또 보다) _______________

**3.** 사과가 맛있어요.

→ (더 사러 가다) _______________

**4.** 비가 와요.

→ (집에 있다) _______________

**5.** 포도가 싸요.

→ (많이 사다) _______________

- 먼저 가 보겠습니다.  I will be going early ("now").

- 먼저 일어나겠습니다.  I will go ("get up") first ("now").

  A formal phrase said to those who will remain if you are the first to leave.

- 더 놀다 오세요.  Enjoy a little while longer.

  Said to those who will remain and enjoy the conversation.

: Korean Insight

# Heungbu Jeon  흥부전

Heungbujeon is a pre-modern work of Korean fiction of unknown authorship. In it there are two brothers. The elder brother, Nolbu, is a bad person with a lot of greed and ambition, not like the younger brother, Heungbu. One day Nolbu kicks Heungbu out of the house because he does not want to share any of their parents' inheritance. Heungbu ends up living in a miserable hut. No matter how hard he works he cannot get enough food to feed his family.

One day he discovers a swallow has built a nest under the eaves of his little hut so as to raise its chicks. When the nest is attacked by a snake, Heungbu gets rid of the attacker, but one of the chicks falls to the ground and its legs are broken. He takes care of the little bird, and so the following year the swallow gives Heungbu a gourd seed. He plants it, and when he breaks open one of the gourds it overflows with gold and silver treasure. Nolbu, hearing that his brother is living happily as a rich man, gets greedy and catches a swallow, breaks its leg, and then tries to help it get better again. Sure enough, the following year Nolbu's swallow brings him a gourd seed. He plants it. Nolbu breaks open one of the gourds, but dokkaebi appeared and took all his wealth away, turning him into a beggar.

It's a typical work of classical Korean fiction, in which the good are met with fortune and the bad are punished. In modern days, however, people often interpret Heungbu to be "incapable" and Nolbu as someone who is "strategizing." The two characters are frequently mentioned allegorically in public debate. What do you think? Is it a story about a good Heungbu and an evil Nolbu, or is it about an "incapable" Heungbu and a "strategizing" Nolbu?

# 거기 리사 씨 집이죠?

Is this Lisa's house?

Track 041

A 여보세요. 거기 리사 씨 집이죠?
B 네, 그런데요.

A   Hello. Is this Lisa's house?
B   Yes, it is.

**Dialogue Tips**

**여보세요.** Hello.
An expression used when making or answering a telephone call.

**네, 그런데요.** Yes, it is.
An expression used in answer to "거기 ○○씨 집이죠?" that is often used as you answer a telephone call.

**Pronunciation Check**   집이죠 [지비조]

**Vocabulary & Expressions**

거기 there, that     씨 suffix used after a person's name, like Mr, Ms.
약속 engagement     댁 house (honorific)     강남역 Gangnam subway station
중국집 a Chinese restaurant

# N-(이)죠?

Used by the speaker when he thinks what he says is correct and seeks affirmation. If the caller wants to confirm that the number he has called is indeed the place he wanted to talk with, he also needs to  use the word '거기'. 'N-(이)죠?' is a shortened form of 'N-(이)지요?'. If the last syllable of the noun ends in a vowel, use '-죠' and if it ends in a consonant, use '-이죠'.

**씨**

Used at the end a person's name as a title of respect, though not one of extreme respect, so you must not use it with the name of someone older than yourself, your teachers, or the head of a company. Be aware of the fact it is never used with only a surname.

- 거기 한국대학교죠? — That's Hanguk University, is it not?
- 약속 시간이 내일 세 시죠? — The appointment is tomorrow at three, right?
- 다음 역이 강남역이죠? — The next station is Gangnam station, right?

# 그런데요

An expression that lets the person who has spoken know you agree with him. It is often used in colloquial speech and often encourages the conversation to continue. In telephone conversations it is often used as part of the response "네, 그런데요." The opposite would be "아닌데요."

- A : 거기 김 선생님 댁이지요? — Is this Mr. Kim's house?
  B : 네, 그런데요. — Yes, it is.

- A : 거기 Arirang TV죠? — Is this Arirang TV?
  B : 아닌데요. — No, it isn't.



**Complete the dialogues, based on the example.**

**Ex.**

A : 거기 리사 씨 집이죠? (리사 씨 집)

B : 네, 그런데요.

1. A : _______________ (서울백화점)

B : 네, 그런데요.

2. A : _______________ (한국대학교)

B : 네, 그런데요.

3. A : _______________ (중국집)

B : 네, 그런데요.

○ **거기 한국대학교입니까?**  Is this Hanguk University?

A more formal expression that shares the same meaning with "거기 한국대학교죠?"

○ **네, 그렇습니다.**  Yes, it is.

A formal expression that has the same meaning as "네, 그런데요."

○ **거기 2345-6789죠?**  Is this 2345-6789?

Used when you want to confirm you have called the right place based on the phone number and not a person or place name.



# Jangdok and Kimchi Refrigerators 장독과 김치냉장고

Do you like any Korean foods? What dish first comes to mind when you think about food from Korea? Surely you must think of kimchi. Kimchi's taste continually changes according to how old it is and the temperature, so you have to store it well if you want to maintain just the right taste. Traditionally kimchi was stored with other fermented foods like soy sauce and soybean pasted in crocks called jangdok.

Made from porcelain clay, they have miniscule air holes that allow air to circulate and aid in fermentation while not allowing the contents to leak. Back in the days before refrigerators, people kept kimchi in jangdok half buried in the ground outdoors in order to maintain the right temperature. People can't use jangdok very easily anymore now that apartment living has become so common, and the answer has been "kimchi refrigerators," produced by a Korean electronic appliance company. It's a special type of refrigerator designed especially for the storage of fermented foods enjoyed by Koreans in a way that maintains their proper taste. As you might imagine, they are very popular. Sounds like quite a lot of effort, doesn't it, the development from "breathing" jangdok to kimchi refrigerators? Koreans do really love their kimchi!

# 네, 전데요.

Yes, that's me.

A  리사 씨 계세요?

B  네, 전데요. 실례지만 누구세요?

A  Is Lisa there?

B  Yes, that's me. Pardon, but who is this?

**OOO 계세요?** Is OOO there?

An expression for asking for someone at a number you have dialed.

**전데요.** That's me.

A shortened form of "저 인데요."

**: Pronunciation** Check

계세요 [계세요/게세요]

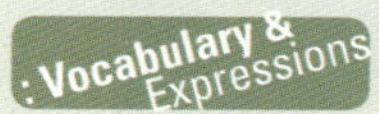
**: Vocabulary &** Expressions

계시다 to be (somewhere, honorific form)        누구 who        서울역 Seoul Station

## –인데요

Means the same as 'N입니다' and 'N이에요/예요', used frequently in conversational speech. It is often used in a context where the conversation is going to continue.

- A: 누구세요?　　　Who is this?
  B: 김영인데요.　　　This is Kim Young.

- A: 저게 뭐예요?　　　What's that?
  B: 63빌딩인데요.　　　That's the 63 Building.

## N-(이)세요?

An honorific form replaces 'N-이에요/예요'. If the last syllable of the noun ends in a vowel, use '-세요' and if it ends in consonant, use '-이세요'.

- 실례지만 누구세요?　　　Excuse me but who might this be?
- 댁이 어디세요?　　　Where do you live?
- 김 선생님이세요?　　　Are you Mr. Kim?

**집/댁, 말/말씀**

For situations when you need to use honorifics in reference to someone, you may also do so with his "house" and "what he said." In such cases use '댁' instead of '집' and '말씀' instead of '말'.

 **Complete the dialogues, based on the example.**

**Ex.**

A: 오늘이 며칠이에요?

B: (15일) **십오 일인데요.**

1. A: 지금 몇 시예요?

   B: (7시) ______________________

2. A: 오늘이 무슨 요일이에요?

   B: (금요일) ______________________

3. A: 여기가 어디예요?

   B: (서울역) ______________________

- **실레지만 어디세요?**  Pardon me, but 'where are you'?

  This question is an indirect way of really asking "who is this?"

- **리사 친구 김영인데요.**  This is Kim Young, a friend of Lisa's.

  A pattern used for explaining who you are.

- **김 선생님 계시면 좀 바꿔 주세요.**  May I please speak to Mr. Kim if he's in?

  An expression you may use to ask for someone if a third person has answered the phone.



# Golgul Temple and Seon Mu Do 골굴사 사찰 체험과 선무도

Have you ever been to Gyeongju? It is an ancient city full of famous landmarks like the temple Bulguksa and the Seokguram Grotto. Unknown to many, Korean Buddhist temples usually end with "sa" at the end of their names, like Golgulsa, a relatively unknown temple in Gyeongju that has a "temple stay" program in which members of the general public can experience temple life by eating temple food, meditating with the monks who live there, learning temple etiquette, and practicing mental discipline.

Golgulsa has a unique form of martial art called Seon Mu Do that has been handed down in Korean temples much like Shaolin Kung Fu has been maintained as a tradition as Shaolin Temple in China. Golgulsa is the Mecca of Seon Mu Do, and if you go there for a "temple stay" there's a special session where you can learn about the art form. Then, how about meditating in a quiet temple, eating delicious food, trying a martial art, and making your body and mind healthier at the same time?

# 잠깐만 기다리세요.

Please wait a moment.

## : Dialogue

A  김영 씨 있으면 좀 바꿔 주세요.
B  잠깐만 기다리세요.

A  May I speak to Mr. Kim Young if he's there?
B  Please wait a moment.

**Dialogue Tips**

**잠깐만 기다리세요.**
**Please wait a moment.**

An expression that tells someone to wait momentarily. You can use it to have someone wait in any situation.

**: Pronunciation Check**

있으면 [이쓰면]

**: Vocabulary & Expressions**

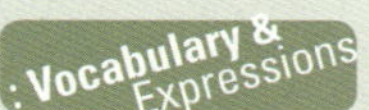

바꾸다 to change, to hand over the phone          잠깐/잠깐만 a little
기다리다 to wait               답 answer          알다 to know, understand
가르치다 to teach, to let someone know something      말하다 to speak, to tell
바꿔 주세요. Please let me speak to him/her.
도와주세요. Please help me.      가르쳐 주세요. Please inform me (of something).

# V¹-(으)면 V²-아/어 주세요

A pattern for asking for something to be done, if conditions are met or require action. For V¹, use '-면' if the verb stem ends in a vowel and '-으면' if it ends in a consonant, except if the consonant is a 'ㄹ', in which case use '-면'. In V², if the verb stem ends in 'ㅏ' or 'ㅗ' use '아' and if it ends in any other vowel use '-어', the exception being that you should use '-해' if it is a '하다' verb.

**바꿔 주세요.**

Here it means "please let me speak to so and so" while talking over the telephone, but since '바꿔' also means "change" or "exchange something" you may also use this expression when asking, for example, that you be allowed to exchange something you have purchased for a different product.

- 김 선생님 계시면 바꿔 주세요.    If Mr. Kim is there, please let me speak to him.

- 필요한 것이 있으면 말해 주세요.   Tell me if you need something.

- 답을 알면 좀 가르쳐 주세요.   Tell me the answer if you know what it is.

   **Complete the dialogues, based on the example.**

**Ex.**

A : 거기 리사 씨 집이죠?
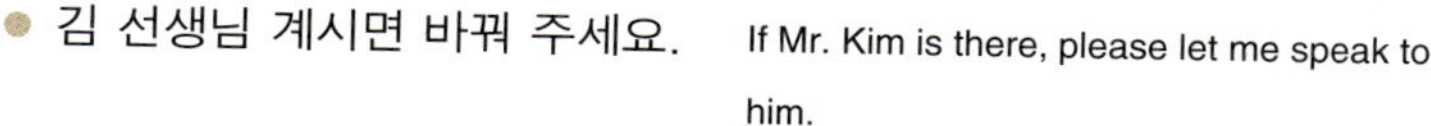

B : 네, 그런데요.

A : 리사 씨 있으면 좀 바꿔 주세요.

B : 전데요.

**1.**

A : (김 선생님 댁)

B : 네, 그런데요.

A :

B : 전데요.

**2.**

A : (김영 씨 집)

B : 네, 그런데요.

A :

B : 잠깐만 기다리세요.

- **잠시만 기다리세요.**  Please wait momentarily.

  This means the same as "잠깐만 기다리세요."

- **잠깐만요. / 잠시만요.**  One moment.

  Short colloquial expressions asking someone to wait.

- **지금 안 계시는데요.**  She/he's not present at the moment.

  This tells the caller that the person he seeks is not available.



# Son Gijeong  손기정

Have you ever heard of Son Gijeong, the Korean marathoner ? He was Korea's first gold medalist in the Olympic marathon, having placed first in the event at the 1936 Olympics in Berlin. Another Korean marathoner, Nam Seungyong won the bronze medal at the same event. Son passed away not too long ago, but to this day he is highly respected by the Korean people as a national hero.

Sadly, however, his win is not recorded in Olympic history as being Korea's first gold. Japan had stolen Korea's sovereignty at the time, so Son had to wear a Japanese uniform when he went to Berlin. The athlete was Korean, but he was a citizen of Imperial Japan. The day Son Gijeong won his gold medal, a Korean newspaper erased the Japanese flag on his uniform from the picture it ran on the front page. That landed members of the newspaper's staff in trouble with the Japanese colonial authorities.

# 잘못 거셨어요.
## You've dialed the wrong number.

Track
044

: Dialogue

A 거기 아리랑 컴퓨터지요?
B 아닌데요. 잘못 거셨어요.
A 죄송합니다.

A Is this Arirang Computer?
B No, it isn't. You've dialed the wrong number.
A I'm sorry.

Dialogue Tips

잘못 거셨어요. You've dialed the wrong number

An expression that tells someone he dialed the wrong number.

죄송합니다.
I'm sorry.

A more polite way to say you're sorry than "미안합니다.", so it is generally best not to shorten it to "죄송해요."

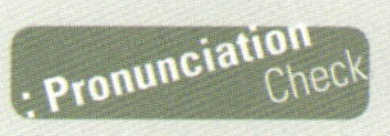
: Pronunciation Check

잘못 거셨어요 [잘몯꺼셔써요]   죄송합니다 [죄송함니다/줴송함니다]

: Vocabulary & Expressions

잘못 error, fault          걸다 to call, dial (telephone)   쓰다 to write
전화번호 telephone number   죄송하다 to be sorry             한국어 Korean language

## 잘못 V

A word describing that something is wrong or mistaken it is widely used in colloquial speech, often when the dialogue is going to continue.

**아닌데요**

This means the same as '아니요' but is frequently used in colloquial speech when it will likely be immediately followed by a response.

- 전화 잘못 거셨어요.    You dialed the wrong number.
- 버스를 잘못 탔어요.    You got on the wrong bus.
- 전화번호를 잘못 말했어요.    I told you the wrong telephone number.

★ Be careful not to confuse '잘못' with '잘 못 V', which expresses how much ability you have at something.

## ㄹ irregular conjugation (Losing the ㄹ)

There are several contexts where verb stems or adjectives ending in 'ㄹ' become exceptions.

❶ When predicative sentence endings lose the 'ㄹ' and have 'ㅂ니다' attached.

- 걸다  →  겁니다

❷ When the stem is in front of '-(으)세요', '-(으)십시오', '-(으)십니다', or '-(으)셨어요', the stem's 'ㄹ' gets left off and the stem goes together with '-세요', '-십시오', '-십니다', and '-셨어요' respectively.

- 만들다 → 만드세요 / 만드십시오 / 만드십니다 / 만드셨어요

❸ When the stem with 'ㄹ' is in front of '-(으)ㄹ 거예요' or '-(으)ㄹ게요', the 'ㄹ' of the stem is omitted so that the stem can fit with '-ㄹ 거예요' or '-ㄹ게요' respectively.

- 살다  →  살 거예요 / 살게요

**Practice**    Complete the dialogues, based on the example.

**Ex.**

A : 이 버스가 512번 버스지요?

B : (타다) 아닌데요. **잘못 타셨어요.**

**1.** A : 거기 리사 씨 집이지요?

B : (걸다) 아닌데요. ___________

**2.** A : 이름이 '김용'이지요?

B : (쓰다) 아닌데요. ___________

**3.** A : 이 책이 한국어 책이지요?

B : (사다) 아닌데요. ___________

○ **실레지만 몇 번에 거셨어요?**  Pardon me but what number did you dial?

You can say this to someone you think may have called you in error, but you want to make sure.

○ **실례지만 어디에 거셨어요?**  Pardon me for asking, but where were you calling?

Say this when you want to make sure your caller has the wrong number.

○ **그런 분 안 계세요.**  There is no such person

An expression for when the caller has telephoned the right number, but the person the caller wishes to talk do is unknown to you.

: Korean Insight

# Garlic  마늘

Along with kimchi, garlic is something that comes to mind when you think about Korea, which probably is one of the largest garlic-devouring countries in the world. It goes into a lot of Korean dishes, and it has a lot of benefits. Garlic has something called "diallyl disulfide," which helps garlic prevent cancer and is said to also slow aging. If you have it with meat it helps digestion and is good for your health. Another helpful effect is that it helps heart and muscle activity and helps maintain the temperature of one's skin by expanding blood vessels.

Garlic is so important that it is one of the main props in one of Korea's foundation myths, since it was the "medicine" that turned a bear into a human being. It is the food product that cannot be done without, and is used in spices and condiments in almost all Korean dishes. You might not like garlic's unique smell, but if only to better your health, why not give Korean food with garlic in it a try sometime?

# 거기 2345-6789 아니에요?

Is this 2345-6789?

Track 045

A  거기 2345-6789 아니에요?
B  아닌데요. 여기는 2345-6780이에요.

A  Is this 2345-6789?
B  No, it isn't. This is 2345-6780.

**Dialogue Tips**

**거기 0000-0000 아니에요?** Is this 0000-0000?

Something you can ask if you're sure you have dialed the correct number.

**아닌데요. 여기는 0000-0000인데요.** No it isn't. This is 0000-0000.

Use this expression to tell a caller what number he has actually dialed.

: **Pronunciation** Check

2345의(-) 6789 [이삼사오에육칠팔구]

: **Vocabulary &** Expressions

아니다 to be not, no   영 zero   박물관 museum
아니에요. (It's) not.

## Reading Phone Numbers

**The numbers you will need for reading telephone numbers are:** 1(일), 2(이), 3(삼), 4(사), 5(오), 6(육), 7(칠), 8(팔), 9(구), **and** 0(영).

Phone numbers can be read in two ways. You can read the number "2345-6789" as '이삼 사오의 육칠팔구', or, alternatively, as '이천삼백사십오 국의 육천칠백팔십구'. These days the former example is more common. The "dash" as pronounced in Korean phone numbers can be spelled out as '의' and pronounced as [에]. However, for mobile phones, people generally omit the '의' and just say the numbers.

★ Traditionally zero is read as [영], but especially when reading a set of numbers, like in a telephone number, it is pronounced [공].

  ● 010-3791-9786 : 공일공 삼칠구일 구칠팔륙

★ In a series of numbers, "6" is pronounced [육] when it is the first syllable, [륙] when it immediately follows a vowel or 'ㄹ' in the preceding syllable, [뉵] when it follows a 'ㅁ', and when it follows a '십(10)' the two are pronounced [심뉵].

## 거기 N이/가 아니에요?

A question you may use, usually without the particle, to confirm again whether you have indeed called the wrong number. Note that you would not use this pattern the first time you are trying to make sure you called the right place.

● 거기 박물관 아니에요?        Is this the museum?
● 거기 김영 씨 집 아니에요?     Is this Kim Young's house?

**Complete the dialogues and read the phone numbers below, based on the example.**

**Ex.**
A : (345-6789)  거기 345-6789 아니에요?

B : (345-6780)
  아닌데요. 여기는 345-6780이에요.

**1.** A : (2343-2344) ___________________

B : (2343-2343)
___________________

**2.** A : (017-363-9807) ___________________

B : (017-364-9807)

**3.** A : (02-889-5488) ___________________

B : (02-880-5488)

○ **거기 한국컴퓨터 아니에요? / 거기 한국컴퓨터 아닌가요?**   Is this Korea Computer?

An expression for asking once again if it is true you have not dialed Korea Computer.
Use it when you have been told the wrong number and you want to make sure you have
the wrong number.

○ **전화번호가 바뀌었어요.**   This phone number has changed. / This is a new number. / She/He has a new number.

An expression you can use to inform the caller that the person he seeks is not at your
number because he has a new phone number.



# Telephone Interpretation Service 통역 서비스 전화

While living in Korea, have you ever found yourself in a predicament because you don't speak enough Korean? If you've ever been in a bind because of your language skills, next time remember to call 1330.

You can dial this number anywhere in the country without a prefix (though you have to dial "02-1330" from a mobile phone) and immediately be connected to a special interpretation service provided by the Korea Tourism Organization for foreign tourists 24 hours a day in English, Japanese, and Chinese. For other languages dial 1588-5644. Volunteers speaking a total of 17 languages are waiting to interpret for you over the phone in urgent situations. Remember this phone number and use it when you're in need.

★ When you find yourself in a real emergency, dial 119 for a police, fire, and ambulance.

# 김 과장님 부탁합니다.

Please let me speak to department director Kim.

: Dialogue

A  김 과장님 부탁합니다.
B  지금 회의 중이신데요.

A  Please let me speak to department director Kim.
B  She's in a meeting right now.

**Dialogue Tips**

**김 과장님 부탁합니다.**
**Please let me speak to department director Kim.**

When asking for a specific person over the telephone, you may use the form "김 과장님 부탁합니다." or, alternatively, you can say "김 과장님 좀 바꿔 주세요."

**부탁합니다** [부타캄니다]   **회의** [회의/회이]

과장 director of a department, section        님 an honorific suffix used at the end of titles
부탁하다 to ask for something, to ask a favor   회의 meeting    난방 heating
문 door    닫다 to close    휴가 vacation        운전 driving    받다 to receive
수업 class, lesson    샤워 shower              부탁합니다. I ask of you.
회의 중이신데요. She/He is in a meeting.

# N 중이신데요

An expression for when someone is in the middle of N. Since you are "elevating" the person you are speaking to 과장님 you need to use honorifics and say 'N 중이신데요' instead of 'N 중이에요' or 'N 중인데요'.

- 지금 회의 중이세요.    That person is currently in a meeting.
- 난방 중입니다. 문을 닫아 주세요.    This building is being heated. Please keep the door closed.
- 지금 휴가 중입니다.    I'm (He/She is) on vacation.

- A : 왜 전화 안 받았어요?    Why didn't you answer the phone?
  B : 운전 중이었어요.    I was in the midst of driving.



**Complete the dialogues, based on the example.**

Ex.

김 과장님 / 회의

A : 김 과장님 부탁합니다.

B : 지금 회의 중이신데요.

1.

리아 씨 / 식사

A : _______________

B : _______________

2.

박 선생님 / 수업

A : _______________

B : _______________

3.

김영 씨 / 샤워

A : _______________

B : _______________

- **지금 통화 중이에요.**  She's busy with another call.

  Say this when you see that someone is occupied with another call.

- **지금 통화 가능해요?**  Can you speak on the telephone right now?
  **지금 전화 받을 수 있어요?**  Can you talk on the phone right now?

  A way to ask the person you have called if he is available to talk.

- **나중에 전화할게요.**  I'll call back later.

  Say this when you are going to call back later.

- **다시 전화 드리겠습니다.**  I will telephone again.

  These can either mean you are going to call again because you have not talked to the right person, or you have talked to the desired person but have reason to inform him you will call again.



# Eunjangdo (the Silver Ornamental Knife) 은장도

An eunjangdo is a knife women would wear on the chest of their clothing during Joseon times. They would carry them as a unique form of self-defense, so as to be able to take their own lives should a man try to violate their chastity. Korean women used to consider chastity as important as life itself, but of course eunjangdo were usually just accessories for traditional clothing. In fact, however, they were used more as symbols of chastity than as actual tools of self defense, because they were often as short as a person's finger and were not very sharp.

These days eunjangdo are produced exclusively as objects of art. They are made of silver and their sheaths might have beautiful engravings or be covered with embroidery work. Because of their beauty and symbolism they are often given as wedding gifts. From now on you should be able to identify an eunjangdo the first time you see one.

# 메모 남기시겠어요?

## Will you leave him/her a message?

**A** 메모 남기시겠어요?
**B** 네, 이름은 김영이고요,
전화번호는 010-2345-6789입니다.

A   Will you leave him/her a message?
B   Good, My name is Kim Young. My phone number is 010-2345-6789.

**메모 남기시겠어요?**
**Will you leave him/her a message?**

A way to ask the person who has answered the phone if he might leave a written message for the person he intended to speak with.

---

**: Pronunciation Check**

남기시겠어요 [남기시게써요]    이름은 [이르믄]

---

**: Vocabulary & Expressions**

메모 memo, a written note    남기다 to leave    취미 hobby
태권도 Taekwondo    카메라 camera    라디오 radio
남기시겠어요? Will you leave (a written message)?

## N¹은/는 N²(이)고요, N³은/는 N⁴입니다.

**An expression for giving successive items of information.**

- 이름은 리사 켈리고요, 전화번호는 010-2345-6789입니다.
  > My name is Lisa Kelly, and my phone number is 010-2345-6789.

- 제 이름은 김영이고요, 취미는 태권도예요.
  > My name is Kim Young and Taekwondo is my hobby.

- 이거는 제 카메라고요, 저거는 친구 라디오예요.
  > This is my camera, and that's my friend's radio.

★ If the noun (in this case a personal name) ends in a vowel you may use either '-이고요' or '-고요', but '-고요' is more common. If it ends in a consonant, use '-이고요'.



**Fill in the appropriate information, based on the example.**

**Ex.**

| | |
|---|---|
| 이름 : 리사 켈리 | |
| 국적 : 미국 | |
| 직업 : 선생님 | |
| 전화번호 : 1234-5678 | |

이름은 리사 켈리고요, 미국 사람이에요.

영어 선생님이고요, 전화번호는 1234-5678이에요.

**1.**

| | |
|---|---|
| 이름 : 왕핑 | |
| 국적 : 중국 | |
| 직업 : 회사원 | |
| 전화번호 : 2345-9876 | |

**2.**

| | |
|---|---|
| 이름 : 이수미 | |
| 국적 : 한국 | |
| 직업 : 학생 | |
| 전화번호 : 3473-2079 | |

- 연락처 하나 주시겠어요?  Can you give me a way how to contact you by phone?

  An expression you can use to ask a person for your phone number?

- 성함과 연락처 주시겠어요?  Can I have your name and contact number?

# Royal Household Vocabulary 왕실 단어

Korea was a country ruled by kings (and, in especially ancient times, by queens) up until as recently as the beginning of the last century, and for that reason the Korean language still has a lot of words and expressions related to royalty, and some are quite interesting. The word yongan, for example, refers to the king's face. Literally, however, it means "dragon face." It would be improper to speak of the face of the king as if it ranked among the commoners, so it was compared to that of a dragon.

The word makes frequent appearances in the famous Korean television dramas "Dae Jang Geum" and "Taejo Wang Geon". In Daejanggeum the character Janggeum works in a "suragan," or a kitchen, which in modern Korean is called a bueok or a jubang. The kitchen Janggeum works in is called a suragan because rice partaken by the king was referred to as sura. Many times words for the king and other royalty were "elevated" in honorific speech by using words for things that existed outside the court but were used exclusively in reference to articles related to the royal household. Have you heard the Korean word, "maehwa"? Literally it refers to the flower of a masil namu, an East Asian plum tree, but the word was also used as a nice word for the king's excrements. Isn't that curious? Listen carefully the next time you watch a television drama where the backdrop is the Korean court in centuries past.

# 리사 집에 있어요?
## Is Lisa at home?

: Dialogue

**A** 저 리사 친구 토미인데요.
리사 집에 있어요?

**B** 지금 자고 있는데요.

A This is Lisa's friend, Tommy. Is Lisa at home?
B She's sleeping at the moment.

**Dialogue Tips**

저 □□ △△인데요.
I'm □□ ('s) △△.

An expression for asking someone who does not know you, if you may speak to a third person at the number you have just called. Put the person you are looking for in □□, and your relationship to □□ in △△.

---

**: Pronunciation Check**   집에 있어요 [지베이써요]   있는데요 [인는데요]

---

**: Vocabulary & Expressions**

| | | |
|---|---|---|
| 자다 to sleep | 숙제하다 to do homework | 언니 elder sister |
| 체육관 gymnasium | 운동하다 to exercise | 거실 living room |
| 비디오 video (tape) | 음악 music | 듣다 to listen, hear |
| 자고 있는데요. (That person is) sleeping. | | |

# N-고 있는데요

You may use this pattern only with a present tense verb. Since the basic pattern is 'V-고 있다' you may also say 'V-고 있어요'. 'V-고 있는데요' is an example of this expression in as colloquial a form as is possible.



**N 중인데요**

This has a similar meaning to "V-고 있는데요", but is used only with gerunds. It has a more formal feel to it than "V-고 있는데요".

- 지금 숙제하고 있는데요.　　She's doing her homework.
- 언니는 지금 체육관에서 운동하고 있는데요.

  My elder sister is exercising at the gymnasium.

- 저는 지금 운전하고 있는데요.　　I'm driving right now.

- A : 동생은 뭐 하고 있어요?　　What is (your/my) younger sibling doing?

  B : 거실에서 비디오 보고 있는데요.　　She/he's watching a video.

- A : 어디 가요?　　Where are you going?

  B : 집에 가는데요.　　I'm going home.

## : Practice

**Complete the following dialogues, based on the example.**

**Ex.**

〈음악 듣다〉

A : 지금 뭐 해요?

B : 음악 듣고 있는데요.

**1.**

〈운전하다〉

A : 지금 뭐 해요?

B : ________________

**2.**

〈신문 읽다〉

A : 지금 뭐 해요?

B : ________________

- **지금 다른 전화 받고 있는데요.**  She/He is on another line right now.

  An expression for telling a caller that the person being sought is busy talking on another telephone line.

- **조금 있다 다시 전화하세요.**  Please call back in a little while.

  Say this to suggest to a caller that she call back later.

- **이따가 다시 전화할게요.**  I'll call back a little later.

  This means you are going to call back later.

: Korean
Insight

# Hwangto (Loess) 황토

Are you trying to have good skin? One of the most important criteria for being beautiful in traditional Korea was clean skin. These days something called "hwangto packs" are a very popular skin care product. "Hwangto packs" are said to be effective in skin moisturizing, whitening, and in the prevention of aging.

Yellow earth is also used in a variety of other ways in Korea. For example, in Boeun, North Chungbuk province, you'll find a place called "Hwangto Villiage" where there's a "hwangto road" covered in "hwangto balls." Aside from being good for the skin, since yellow dirt emitts for infrared rays, when you come in contact with it your skin relaxes and toxins are discharged from the body. It's the reason why hwangto-based jjimjilbang, a type of sauna, has rooms made from yellow dirt and it's what makes them so popular. How about trying a hwangto pack on your skin sometime soon?

# 전화 좀 받아 주세요.

Please get the phone.

Track
049

A  리사 씨, 전화 좀 받아 주세요.

B  못 받아요. 지금 통화 중이에요.

A  Lisa, please get the phone. (Take the phone.)
B  I can't. I'm on (another) phone right now.

**Dialogue Tips**

**전화 좀 받아 주세요.**
**Please get the phone.**

A way to ask someone else to answer the phone when you are unable to answer it yourself.

**: Pronunciation Check**

받아 주세요 [바다주세요]    못 받아요 [몯빠다요]

**: Vocabulary & Expressions**

| | | |
|---|---|---|
| 통화 telephone conversation | 회사 company | −도 too, also, even |
| 연락처 a place (way) to contact someone (email, phone, etc) | 미안하다 to be sorry | |
| 손 hand | 아프다 to hurt, be sick | 이따가 in a short while |
| 생일 birthday | 아르바이트 part time working | 놀다 to play |

받아 주세요. Please get/take (the phone).

통화 중이에요. She/He is busy (on the phone)./I am busy (on the phone).

# 못 V

A form of negation. It expresses that is not possible and can only be used with a verb.



**안 V / 못 V**

'안 V' and '못 V' are both forms of negation, but '안 V' implies the non-action relates to personal choice whereas '못 V' means you are unable to do an action for reasons that are not your choice.

- 오늘은 회사에 못 가요.      I can't go to work today.

- 어제 운동을 못했어요. 오늘도 못해요.

  I was unable to exercise yesterday. I won't be able to today, either.

- A: 태권도를 할 수 있어요?      Can you do any Taekwondo?

  B: 아뇨, 못해요.      No, I can't.

- A : 여기에 연락처 좀 써 주세요.      Write down your contact information here.

  B : 미안해요. 못 써요. 손이 아파요.      I'm sorry. I can't write. My hand hurts.

- A : 이따가 저녁 같이 먹어요.      Let's eat together in a little bit.

  B : 미안해요. 같이 못 먹어요. 오늘 동생 생일이에요.

       Sorry. I can't eat with you. Today is my younger sibling's birthday.

: Practice     **Complete the dialogues, based on the example.**

**Ex.**

A : 우리 오늘 한국어 공부 같이 해요.

B : 미안해요. <u>못해요.</u> 바빠요.

**1.** A : 오후에 같이 산에 가요.

B : 미안해요. ___________ 숙제가 많아요.

**2.** A : 이따가 같이 저녁 먹어요.

B : 미안해요. ___________ 아르바이트 가요.

**3.** A : 전화 받으세요.

B : 미안해요. ___________ 샤워 중이에요.

**4.** A : 내일 같이 영화 봐요.

B : 미안해요. ___________ 약속이 있어요.

**5.** A : 오늘 저녁에 같이 놀아요.

B : 미안해요. ___________ 일이 많아요.

○ **지금 통화 중인데요. 기다리시겠어요?**  He's on the phone right now. Would you like to wait?

When a caller wants to speak with someone who is busy talking on another line, the person who answered the phone may use this expression to inform the caller of the present situation.

○ **그럼 메모 남길게요.**  Then I'd like to leave a message for him.

This means you'd like to have the person answering the phone write a note to the person you intended to speak with.

# Electronic Public Documents 전자민원서류

Getting a passport made or selling and buying a home requires a lot of official documentation. Thanks to an all-out IT (information technology) push on the part of the government, nowadays in Korea you can take care of most of the required paperwork without leaving your home.

"Electronic government" is the term given an online system through which citizens can take care of everything from simple personal legal paperwork to major administrative transactions over the internet. Take the time to visit Korea's "electronic government" site, www.egov.go.kr and you will be able to see an amazingly wide range of documents available, including those relevant to foreigners living in Korea. Many countries have similar programs, but a study by Brown University in the USA cited Korea as the world's top-ranking country in the area of electronic government. Korea has been exporting its know-how in this area to Japan, Russia, Rumania, and, on a smaller scale, cities and police agencies in countries around the world. Things are going to be a lot more convenient in the future.

# 크게 좀 말씀해 주세요.

**Please speak a little louder.**

## : Dialogue

A  잘 안 들려요. 크게 좀 말씀해 주세요.

B  여보세요. 잘 들리세요?

A  I can't hear you very well. Please speak a little louder.
B  Hello. Can you hear me (now)?

> **Dialogue Tips**
>
> **잘 안 들려요. I can't hear you very well.**
>
> Say this when you can hear the other person but not clearly enough to make out what is being said.

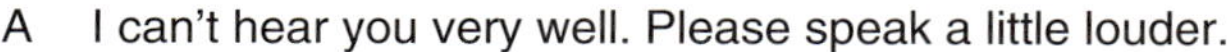

**: Pronunciation Check**

잘 안 들려요 [잘 안들려요]

**: Vocabulary & Expressions**

| | |
|---|---|
| 잘 들리다 to sound (be heard) well | 소리 sound  너무 too |
| 글씨 handwriting, penmanship | 예쁘게 prettily, beautifully |
| 나오다 to have something come out (picture, result) | 더럽다 to be dirty |
| 깨끗하다 to be clean | 덥다 to be hot (weather) |
| 시원하다 to be cool, refreshing (weather) | 가볍다 to be light |
| 들려요. I can hear you. | 말씀해 주세요. Please go ahead (and speak). |

# A-게

'-게' is added to an adjective stem to make an adverb. The created word, thus, must be followed by a verb.

- 소리가 너무 작아요. 크게 말해 주세요.

  The sound is too small. Please speak louder.

- 맛있게 먹었습니다.    I ate deliciously. (I enjoyed the meal.)

- 이 사진 좀 보세요. 아주 예쁘게 나왔어요.

  Look at this photograph. It came out very prettily.

**크게 좀 말씀해 주세요.**
Please speak a little louder.

Say this when you can barely hear the person on the other end of the line.

# 잘 안 들려요.

In its original form, '들려요' is '들리다', the passive form of '듣다'. It cannot be used with the negative '못'.

- 소리가 잘 안 들려요.    I can't hear you very well.
- 글씨가 잘 안 보여요.    I can't see the writing very well.

★ '보이다' is the passive form of '보다'.

 **Make sentences, based on the example.**

(더럽다 ↔ 깨끗하다)  옷이 너무 더러워요. *좀 깨끗하게 해 주세요.*

1. (크다 ↔ 작다)    소리가 너무 커요. ________________

2. (덥다 ↔ 시원하다)  방이 너무 더워요. ________________

3. (무겁다 ↔ 가볍다)  가방이 너무 무거워요. ________________

- **좀 작게 해 주세요.** *Please turn down the volume.*

  A way to request that the volume be turned down.

- **맛있게 해 주세요.** *Please make it tasty.*

  Say this when ordering food and you want the establishment to make your order especially delicious.

: Korean Insight

# Traditional Knots 전통매듭

Go to any place in Korea that sells tourist souvenirs and you'll see traditional Korean knots designed as products such as mobile phone accessories and key chains. In traditional times knots were used on formal clothing and for various decorative purposes. Traditional shapes include triangular knots, knots in the shape of butterflies, plum blossom knots, and many more.

Korean knots are hard to learn from merely looking at them or studying historical records, so the knowledge of how to tie them has long been handed down from person to person, from hand to hand, through the generations. In Joseon times they were very popular as decorations on traditional clothes, as personal accessories, and even on everyday household items. Today traditional knots are often taught in classes open to the public, in places like "cultural centers" run by large department stores. They make fine gifts; why don't you take the time to learn how to tie Korean knots so you can give them to your friends?

# 남산에 가 본 적 있어요?

Have you ever been to Namsan?

Track
051

**A** 남산에 가 본 적 있어요?

**B** 네, 한 번 가 봤어요.

A Have you ever been to Namsan?

B Yes, I've been once.

**Dialogue Tips**

**OO에 가 본 적 있어 요?** Have you ever been to OO?

A question asking someone if he has had the experience of going to a particular location.

**Pronunciation Check**  남산에 [남사네]    가 본 적 있어요 [가본저기써요]    가 봤어요 [가봐써요]

**Vocabulary & Expressions**  남산 Namsan ("Mount Nam," usually said as just "Namsan," a mountain in downtown Seoul)
제주도 Jeju Island　　　　꺅두기 kkakdugi　　　　에게 to, at, for
선물하다 to give a gift　　　스키 ski

## V-(으)ㄴ 적(이) 있어요?

A way to inquire about a person's experience. It is also frequently combined with the pattern 'V-아/어 보다' or 'V-아/어 본 적(이) 있어요?'. The particle '이' often gets omitted.

**V-아/어 보다**

This means "to try doing something you haven't tried previously."

● 한국 음식을 만들어 본 적이 있어요?

Have you ever made Korean food before?

● 친구에게 꽃을 선물한 적 있어요?　　Have you ever given a friend flowers?

● A : 깍두기 먹어 본 적 있어요?　　Have you ever tried kkakdugi?

　 B : 아뇨, 없어요.　　No, I haven't (had that experience).

★ The declarative form is 'V-아/어 본 적(이) 있어요'.

● 제주도에 가 본 적이 있어요.　　I have been to Jeju Island.

● 미국에 가 본 적이 있어요.　　I have been to America.

★ If the verb stem ends in a vowel use '-ㄴ 적', and if it ends in a consonant, say '-은 적'. If it ends with a 'ㄹ', however, omit the 'ㄹ' and use '-ㄴ 적'.

## : Practice　　**Complete the dialogues, based on the example.**

**Ex.**

(제주도에 가 보다)

A : 제주도에 가 본 적 있어요?

B : 네, 가 봤어요.

**1.** (깍두기를 먹어 보다)

A : ____________________

B : 네, 먹어 봤어요.

**2.** (이 노래를 들어 보다)

A : ____________________

B : 아뇨, 못 들어 봤어요.

**3.** (스키를 타 보다)

A : ____________________

B : 네, 있어요.

**4.** (태권도를 배우다)

A : ____________________

B : 네, 있어요.

**5.** (가수를 만나다)

A : ____________________

B : 아뇨, 없어요.

- A : 남산에 가 봤어요?  Have you ever been to Namsan?

  B : 네, 한 번 가 본 적 있어요.  Yes, I've been there once.

  Both forms express experience, and are interchangeable.

- A : 여기에 와 본 적 있어요?  Have you ever been here?

  B : 아니요, 처음인데요.  No, this is the first time.

  An expression for telling someone, in response to a question, that you have never been to the location in question before.

: Korean Insight

# Sanjeok (Korean Food) 산적

Galbi, bulgogi, and bibimbap are well recognized Korean dishes. But have you ever heard about sanjeok? The word refers to food cooked on skewers, which are called kkochi. There are many varieties. Yukjeok is beef on skewers. Then there is eojeok is marinated fish, and sojeok, which consists of skewered mushroom, tofu, green onion, garlic, and other vegetables.

Skewered foods are a common part of everyday meals but are essential dishes for traditional rituals such as sacrifices for ancestors (jesa) and the formal introduction of a bride to her new parents-in-law immediately following a wedding ceremony. Sanjeok does not have a particularly long history as part of Korean cuisine, but it is pretty and one of the foods people like to entertain guests with. In addition to looking nice, it's also easy to make! Try making some the next time you cook for friends.

# 지하철로 가면 금방이에요.

### It's right there if you go by subway.

**A** 여기에서 멀어요?

**B** 아뇨, 지하철로 가면 금방이에요.

A   Is it far from here?
B   No, it's right there if you go by subway.

**지하철로 가면 금방이
에요.** It's right there if
you go by subway.

An expression for saying it
does not take long to get to
a given place by subway.

멀어요 [머러요]

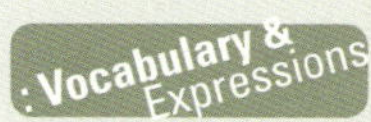

금방 just, right, now, just a moment

# N(으)로 가면 금방이에요

A sentence pattern that means it is not far or does not take long to arrive at the desired location.

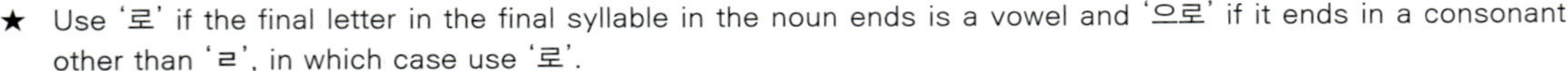

- 버스로 가면 금방이에요.　　It's just a little ways by bus.

- A : 시간이 없어요.　　We don't have time.
  B : 괜찮아요. 지하철로 가면 금방이에요.
  　　Don't worry. We'll be there shortly if we take the subway.

- A : 오토바이로 가면 금방이지요? It's right there if you go by motorcycle, right?
  B : 네, 5분쯤 걸려요.　　Yes, it takes about five minutes.

★ Use '로' if the final letter in the final syllable in the noun ends is a vowel and '으로' if it ends in a consonant other than 'ㄹ', in which case use '로'.

- 비행기로, KTX로, 지하철로

**N(으)로 가다**

An expression for talking about what kind of transportation is being used to get somewhere. A similar expression would be 'N을/를 타고 가다'.

: Practice　Complete the dialogues below, based on the example.

Ex.

A : 여기에서 멀어요?

B : 아뇨, 택시로 가면 금방이에요.

1.

A : 여기에서 가까워요?

B : 네, 

2.

A : 여기에서 멀어요?

B : 아뇨, 

● 여기에서 금방이에요.  It's just a little ways from here.

● 별로 멀지 않아요.  It's not that far.

● A : 걸어가면 한참 걸려요?  Does it take long if I walk?
B : 아뇨, 금방이에요.  No, it's right close.



# Yeotchigi (the Taffy Breaking Game) 엿치기

Have you ever tried yeot? It's a Korean candy similar to taffy. Back in the days when there was little in the way of sweet snacks it was very popular. There is a game of sorts associated with it called yeotchigi which involves breaking hard yeot into pieces and seeing whose piece of yeot has the most holes and which piece is larger. The person who loses in the game is supposed to pay for the yeot that has just been broken. Some people are quite good at it, and, they say, know how to blow into a broken piece of yeot and make the holes bigger.

Doesn't that sound like fun? Back in the old days people knew how to get the most fun out of something simple like sweets and snacks. These days it can be hard to find places that sell yeot, but you're sure to find some if you go to Seoul's Insa-dong or the Korean Folk Village. When you get the chance to try yeot, be sure to try your hand at yeotchigi with your friends.

# 한 시간쯤 걸릴 거예요.

## It should take about an hour.

A  오래 걸려요?
B  한 시간쯤 걸릴 거예요.

A  Does it take long?
B  It should take about an hour.

**Dialogue Tips**

**오래 걸려요?**
**Does it take long?**

A way to ask if a lot of time must first elapse before a given action comes to completion.


**걸릴 거예요** [걸릴꺼예요]

| | | |
|---|---|---|
| 오래 long (time) | 들 plural suffix | 늦다 to be late |
| 아이 child | 아마 maybe | 모자라다 to be short, insufficient |
| 충분하다 to be enough | 춥다 to be cold | 잘 well |
| 맞다 to fit | | |

# A/V-(으)ㄹ 거예요

This expresses conjecture, usually of a subjective nature. You can use it when you feel sure but don't have an authoritative basis. It works with both verbs and adjectives, often together with the adverb '아마'.

- 한 시간쯤 걸릴 거예요.　　It should take about an hour.
- 지금 떠나면 안 늦을 거예요.　　We won't be late if we leave now.
- 아이는 아마 자고 있을 거예요.　　The child is surely sleeping right now.

> **Grammar Tips**
>
> **V-(으)ㄹ 거예요**
>
> This expresses the future tense or that which is expected. It works only with vowels, and can be used also as an interrogative expression.

★ This expression can assume the interrogative form; 'A/V-(으)ㄹ까요?'

- A : 사람들이 많이 올까요?　　Are a lot of people going to come?
- B : 네, 많이 올 거예요.　　Yes, many will be coming.

★ If the final syllable in the verb stem ends in a vowel, use '-ㄹ 거예요'. If it ends in a consonant, use '-을 거예요', unless it ends in a 'ㄹ', in which cause omit the 'ㄹ' and use '-ㄹ 거예요'.

## Practice

**Make sentences, based on the example.**

**Ex.**

A : 사람들이 많이 올까요?

B : 네, **많이 올 거예요.**
　　(많이 오다)

**1.** A : 음식이 모자랄까요?

B : 아뇨, _______________
　　(충분하다)

**2.** A : 아이가 자고 있을까요?

B : 네, _______________
　　(자고 있다)

**3.** A : 내일 더울까요?

B : 아뇨, _______________
　　(춥다)

**4.** A : 많이 늦어요?

B : 네, _______________
　　(한 시간쯤 늦다)

**5.** A : 이 원피스가 작을까요?

B : 아뇨, _______________
　　(잘 맞다)

- **얼마나 걸릴까요?**  How long should it take?

  An expression for asking how long a given activity will require.

- **좀 오래 걸릴 거예요.**  It will take a while.

  This tells someone that it won't take long, but it's not going to happen immediately either.

- **아마 그럴 거예요.**  Probably that is the case.

  Use this to tell someone that you agree with what he just said because he is probably correct.



# Korean Temples 한국의 사찰

Korea was once officially a Buddhist nation, and for hundreds of years. Have you ever been to a temple (jeol, sachal)? Did you feel your mind become calmer? Buddhist temples are places were monks practice the way of Buddhism and teach its principles. Their beauty is to be found in the way their charming buildings are in harmony with nature. There are many famous temples.

One among them is Jikjisa, or Jikji Temple, first built some 1,600 years ago. Much of it burned down during war and so it is not what it used to be, but even now it is famous for its beauty. Buseoksa, or Buseok Temple, is famous for one of its buildings, Muryangsu Jeon which is National Treasure #18 and is recognized for its very unique pillar design. Perhaps Korea's most famous temple of all is Bulguksa, or Bulguk Temple, in Gyeongju, North Gyeongsang Province. There you'll see some of the finest pagodas that remain today, both of which are also designated national treasures. Korea's Buddhist temples are not grandiose in terms of their scale, but their refined and subtle harmony with their natural surroundings seem to put their visitors' minds at ease. Be sure to visit some of Korea's finest temples should you get the chance.

# 한 번 갈아타야 돼요.

You have to transfer once.

Track
054

A  한 번에 갈 수 있어요?

B  아뇨, 한 번 갈아타야 돼요.

A  Can I go all in one (ride)?
B  No, you have to transfer once.

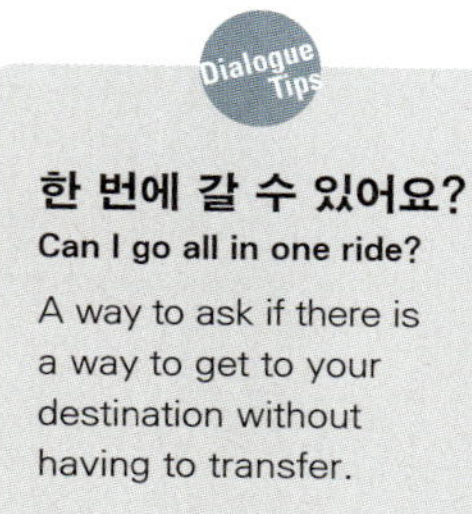

**Dialogue Tips**

**한 번에 갈 수 있어요?**
**Can I go all in one ride?**

A way to ask if there is
a way to get to your
destination without
having to transfer.

---

**: Pronunciation Check**

갈 수 있어요 [갈쑤이써요]    갈아타야 돼요 [가라타야돼요/뒈요]

**: Vocabulary & Expressions**

한번 once, one time            갈아타다 to transfer (bus, plane, subway)

교수 professor                 청소하다 to clean

꼭 necessarily, surely, exactly    약 medicine

내다 to pay                    갈아타야 돼요. You have to transfer (buses, etc.).

# A/V-아/어야 돼요

This expression means that something must happen, as it expresses duty, obligation, or how things should be.

- 오늘은 교수님을 만나야 돼요.　　I have to meet my professor today.

- 늦으면 안 돼요. 약속 시간 10분 전까지 와야 돼요.
  　　　　You can't be late. You must be there ten minutes before the agreed time.

- A : 약을 꼭 먹어야 돼요?　　Do I absolutely have to take medicine?

  B : 네, 먹어야 돼요.　　Yes, you have to take medicine.

★ If the verb (or adjective) stem ends in the vowels 'ㅏ' or 'ㅗ', add '-아 돼요'. If it is a '하다' verb (or adjective) the '하' of '하다' verb becomes '해' to form '-해야 돼요'. In all other instances, use '-어야 돼요'.

- 가다 → 가야 돼요　　　청소하다 → 청소해야 돼요　　　읽다 → 읽어야 돼요

★ 'A/V-아/어야 돼요' is often the answer to questions posed as 'V-(으)면 돼요?' or 'V-아/어도 돼요?'.

- A : 8시까지 오면 돼요? / 8시까지 와도 돼요?　Will it do if I'm there by 8 o'clock? / Is it okay if I'm back by 8 o'clock?

  B : 아뇨, 7시까지 와야 돼요.　　No, you have to come (back) by 7 o'clock.

 **Practice**　　**Make sentences, based on the example.**

**Ex.**

A : 6시까지 오면 돼요?

B : 아뇨, 5시까지 와야 돼요.　　(5시)

1. A : 오백 원 내면 돼요?

   B : 아뇨, ＿＿＿＿＿＿＿＿＿＿＿＿＿＿＿ (천 원)

2. A : 53과까지 공부하면 돼요?

   B : 아뇨, ＿＿＿＿＿＿＿＿＿＿＿ (54과)

3. A : 여기서 갈아타면 돼요?

   B : 아뇨, ＿＿＿＿＿＿＿＿＿＿＿ (저기)

○ **한 번에 못 가요?**  I can't get there in just one ride?

Use this expression to ask if you really have to transfer.

○ **A : 여기서부터 가는 게 복잡해요?**  Is the way to get there complicated?

　**B : 아뇨, 간단해요.**  No, it's simple.

Question A is a way to ask if getting to your destination is complicated. B is an answer to question A, meaning that the way to get there is not complicated.

○ **A : 몇 번 갈아타야 돼요?**  How many times do I have to transfer?　　　**B : 한 번요.**  Once.

Question A is a way to ask how many times you have to transfer. B is a simple expression, which means if you transfer one time, you can get to your destination.

: Korean Insight

# Kongjwi Patjwi Jeon 콩쥐팥쥐전

Do you know the ancient story Kongjwi and Patjwi? It is originally a work of classical Korean prose fiction titled "Kongjwi Patjwi Jeon." Think of it as Korea's version of "Cinderella."

Once upon a time a loving husband and his wife had a pretty little baby girl named Kongjwi. As she was growing up, however, her mother died of disease and her father remarried a woman with a daughter by the name of Patjwi. Kongjwi's stepmother mistreated her, but she was a good child and endured anyway. One day there was a party at Kongjwi's relatives' house. Kongjwi told her stepmother she would be going, but her stepmother said that instead she and her daughter Patjwi would be going and that Kongjwi would have to stay behind and do extra chores like weaving. Kongjwi was crying about being unable to visit her maternal mother's relatives when a fairy descended from the heavens and weaved to make fine clothing and shoes for her. Kongjwi tried them on and went to her relatives'. On her way she noticed a local aristocrat going down the road, and wanting to avoid him, she moved away. One of her shoes fell off, however, and the two married and lived happily ever after the aristocrat found the shoe's owner.

The story sure sounds like Cinderella? A lot of ancient Korean stories have plots that are somewhat universal.

# 몇 호선을 타야 돼요?
## What subway line do I have to take?

**A** 몇 호선을 타야 돼요?

**B** 2호선을 타고 가다가 교대역에서 내리세요.

A  What subway line do I have to take?
B  Take (Seoul subway) Line 2 and get off at Gyodae.

**몇 호선을 타야 돼요?**
**What subway line do I have to take?**

This is how you ask what number subway line to take.

**O호선을 타고 가다가 OO역에서 내리세요.**
**Take line number O and get off at OO station.**

Say this to someone if you tell him what line to take and where to get off instead of going to the end of the line.



몇 호선을 [며토서늘]　　2호선을 [이호서늘]　　교대역에서 [교대여게서]

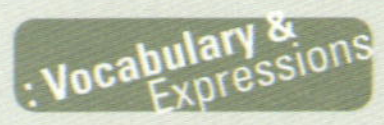

호선 line number　　　2호선 subway line #2　　　교대역 Gyodae subway station
울다 to cry　　　들르다 to drop in, stop by　　　쇼핑하다 to shop

## V¹-다가 V²

This expresses that action $V^2$ begins to take place before action $V^1$ is complete, or that $V^2$ begins to happen while $V^1$ is still in progress.

- 숙제하다가 잤어요.  ⠀⠀I fell asleep while doing homework.
- 밥 먹다가 전화를 받았어요.  ⠀⠀I was eating when I took a phone call.
- 음악 듣다가 잤어요.  ⠀⠀I fell asleep while listening to music.
- 집에 가다가 슈퍼에 잠깐 들를 거예요.  I'm going to stop by the supermarket on my way home.
- 책을 읽다가 지하철을 놓쳤어요.  I was reading a book when I missed the subway.

★ Tense is not applied to $V^1$ in '$V^1$-다가 $V^2$'. You can determine whether the action belongs in the present, past or future by the sentence ending that follows $V^2$.

- 밥 먹다가 잤어요.  ⠀⠀I slept while eating.
- 집에 가다가 전화할 거예요.  ⠀⠀I will call while going home.

    **Make sentences, based on the example.**

**Ex.** 숙제하다 + 자다

→ 숙제하다가 잤어요.

**1.** 회사에 가다 + 친구를 만나다

→

**2.** 책을 읽다 + 전화 받다

→

**3.** 영화 보다 + 울다

→

**4.** 쇼핑하다 + 선생님을 만나다

→

**5.** 집에 가다 + 전화하다

→

- **몇 호선이 거기에 가요?**  What subway line (number) goes there?

  A way to ask what subway line to take.

- **어느 역에서 내려요?**  What station do I get off at?

  **어느 역에서 내려야 돼요?**  What station do I have to get off at?

  These are ways to ask what station to get off the subway at.

- **몇 호선 (지하철) 타요?**  What (subway) line should I take?

  An expression for asking what number subway line to take.

- **몇 번 (버스) 타요?**  What number (bus) should I take?

  An expression for asking what number bus to take.



# Kimchi Jjigae 김치찌개

Kimchi jjigae is surely one of the dishes Koreans eat most, and its main ingredient is none other than kimchi. There can be a lot of variety in kimchi jjigae, depending on what you put in it. There's chamchi kimchi jjigae, which is kimchi jjigae with tuna in it. If you add yubu it becomes yubu kimchi jjigae. Add uncurled bean curd and it becomes sundubu kimchi jjigae. Koreans think they've had an ample meal if they've just got their kimchi jjigae, even if there aren't the side dishes you usually see with Korean meals.

It is simple to make. Squeeze cabbage-based kimchi to remove most of its liquid, cut it in 5 centimeter lengths and boil it in water with finely sliced pork. Taste it once you've let it boil for a while, then either add more "kimchi juice" or hot pepper paste. Once you're done add sliced green onion. Usually the initial kimchi itself is enough to get the right taste. Koreans think that a serving of kimchi jjigae and steamed rice is all you need for a simple meal in the cold of winter. Be sure to try making it at home sometime.

# 거기서 몇 호선으로 갈아타야 돼요?

What number line do I have to transfer to from there?

Track 056

A 거기서 몇 호선으로 갈아타야 돼요?

B 3호선으로 갈아타면 돼요.

A What number line do I have to transfer to from there?

B Transfer to Line #3.

**Dialogue Tips**

**거기서 몇 호선으로 갈아타야 돼요?**

**What number line do I transfer to from there?**

A way for someone being given information about how to get somewhere to ask what line he has to transfer to.

**: Pronunciation Check**

몇 호선으로 [며토서느로]    3호선으로 [삼호서느로]*

갈아타면 돼요 [가라타면돼요/돼요]

*Here the "ㅎ" gets pronounced softly.

**: Vocabulary & Expressions**

3호선 Subway Line #3        (으)로 (over) to

4호선 Subway Line #4        8호선 Subway Line #8        1호선 Subway Line #1

# N(으)로 갈아타다

**Use this expression to talk about how or where to transfer, to go on the way to your destination.**

**N(으)로**

This has many meanings, but in this chapter it is used to express the direction of change.

- 다음 역에서 2호선으로 갈아타세요.   Transfer Line #2 at the next station.
- 버스를 타고 가다가 지하철로 갈아탔어요.

  I took a bus, then got on the subway.
- A : 어디에서 갈아타야 해요?   Where do I have to transfer?

  B : 교대역에서 3호선으로 갈아타세요.   Transfer at Gyodae Station to Line #3.



**Read the subway map below and make sentences, based on the example.**

**Ex.**

(교대역, 3호선)

A : 몇 호선으로 갈아타야 돼요?

B : 교대역에서 3호선으로 갈아타면 돼요.

**1.**

(사당역, 4호선)

A : 몇 호선으로 갈아타야 돼요?

B : ________________________________

**2.**

(잠실역, 8호선)

A : 몇 호선으로 갈아타야 돼요?

B : ________________________________

**3.**

(시청역, 1호선)

A : 몇 호선으로 갈아타야 돼요?

B : ________________________________

○ **홍콩에서 한국 비행기로 갈아탔어요.** I transferred to a Korean plane (airline) in Hong Kong.

This expression says that you got off one plane and got on another, one that flies under a different flag.

○ **내려서 몇 호선으로 갈아타야 돼요?** What number line do I have to transfer to after I get off?

An expression for asking what you need to take next, after you get off the line you are currently riding.

○ **어디까지 왔어요?** How far have you come?

Someone you plan to meet at your destination might ask you this over the phone.

○ **이제 막 2호선으로 갈아탔어요.** I've just transferred to Line #2.

An expression that tells someone on the phone that you've just transferred to Line #2.



# Onomatopoeia and Exclamations 의성어와 감탄사

Every language has ways to imitate the sound of a clock ticking or the sounds animals make. Korean has an especially wide variety of onomatopoeia. Korean chicken (dak) go "kkokkio." Guess what sound Korean pigs (dwaeji) make? They go "kkul kkul," which is why pigs sometimes get called "kkulkkuri." The sound of a dog (gae) barking is "meong meong" and so sometimes people call dogs meong meongi.

Guns make a sound "tang tang," a clock ticking is "jjaekkak jjaekkak," and a doorbell makes the sound "ding dong."

When Koreans try to tell others to be quiet, they place an index finger over their lips and quietly say "swit." Don't be startled if swit sounds like a certain word in English. It's not vulgarity.

Also, when Koreans get hurt, they say "aya!" like when an English speaker says "ouch!"

# 별로 복잡하지 않아요.

It's not that complicated.

**A** 너무 복잡해요.

**B** 아니에요. 별로 복잡하지 않아요.

A  That's too complicated.

B  No. It's not that complicated.

**Dialogue Tips**

**별로 복잡하지 않아요.**
It's not that complicated.

Because the word '복잡하다' has two meanings, this expression means there are not that many people or that some matter or procedure is not too much of a headache. In this chapter we will use it for the latter meaning.

**: Pronunciation** Check
복잡해요 [복짜패요]   복잡하지 않아요 [복짜파지아나요]

**: Vocabulary & Expressions**

별로 not especially      복잡하다 to be complicated      시험 test

일 work, a matter, issue      힘들다 to be difficult      싱겁다 to be (taste) flat, bland

# 별로 A-지 않아요

An expression meaning the degree of something is not all that notable or serious. Note that while '별로' means "especially" or "particularly," it is always used as part of a negative, as if it were the "especially" in the phrase "not especially." This expression works with verbs, but some verbs may require being accompanied by an adverb.

- 길이 별로 복잡하지 않아요.　　The road is not that complicated. / There isn't that much traffic.
- 시험이 별로 어렵지 않았어요.　　The test is not that bad.
- 방이 별로 깨끗하지 않아요.　　The room isn't all that clean.

- A : 여기서 멀어요?　　Is it far from here?
  B : 아뇨, 별로 멀지 않아요.　　No, it isn't so far.

- A : 일이 힘들지요?　　The work is hard, right?
  B : 아뇨, 별로 힘들지 않아요.　　No, it isn't that difficult.

★ 'A/V-지 않다' is a long form of negation that attaches directly to the stem of a verb or adjective regardless of whether the stem has a final consonant or not. Its formal form is '-지 않습니다' and its informal form is '-지 않아요'. The short form of this same type of negative phrase would be '안 A/V'.



**Complete the dialogues, based on the example.**

Ex.
A : 길이 복잡해요?

B : 아뇨, 별로 복잡하지 않아요.

1. A : 여기서 멀어요?

   B : 아뇨, _______________

2. A : 일이 힘들어요?

   B : 아뇨, _______________

3. A : 옷이 비싸요?

   B : 아뇨, _______________

4. A : 오늘 더워요?

   B : 아뇨, _______________

5. A : 음식이 싱거워요?

   B : 아뇨, _______________

- **별로예요.** Not especially. / I don't feel like it.

  A very colloquial way to say the quality or state of something is not very good.

- **그렇게 복잡하지는 않아요.** It's not that complicated (crowded).

  This means something is not that complicated (or crowded), but also that it could be just a little.

# The Significance of Half an Egg 계란 반쪽의 의미

Have you ever heard of naengmyeon? The name literally means "cold noodles." You really want to have some when it gets hot in summer, though they say it is supposed to be eaten in winter. There are largely two types, the spicy hot bibim naengmyeon and another variety called mul naengmyeon, which has a refreshingly cool broth.

Naengmyeon always seems to have half a boiled egg in it. Have you ever wondered why? It's to protect your stomach. The noodles in naengmyeon are made from buckwheat and flour, and since buckwheat has cellulose in it you can damage your stomach if you eat it when your stomach is otherwise empty. That half an egg serves to keep your stomach occupied. You'll find eggs in other Korean noodle dishes as well for the same reason. Korean food does not involve courses, so the egg serves to excite the appetite and protect your stomach in a country where there aren't usually appetizers. It also makes the noodles look pretty. The next time you have naengmyeon, be sure to have your egg first.

# 나가면 바로 보여요.

It's visible right after you exit (the station).

Track
058

A 지하철역에서 가까워요?
B 네, 나가면 바로 보여요.

A Is it nearby the subway station?
B Yes, it's visible right after you exit (the station).

**Dialogue Tips**

**나가면 바로 보여요.**
**It's visible right after you exit (the station).**

This tells someone the place he is looking for is very close by once he goes outside.

: **Pronunciation** Check

지하철역 [지하철력]　　지하철역에서 [지하철려게서]

: **Vocabulary & Expressions**

나가다 to exit　　　　　　바로 right, immediately　　　출구 an exit
정문 front gate/entrance　들어오다 to enter　　　　신청하다 to apply
보이다 to be seen, be visible　서랍 drawer　　　　　　열다 to open
있다 to be, exist

## V-(으)면 바로 보여요

A phrase commonly used in the course of finding a place or thing, meaning that you should be able to see it once you do something.

**바로 V**

This pattern is used to mean something is not complicated and roundabout or does not involve a lot of time.

- 3번 출구로 나가면 바로 보여요.   It is seeable right after you leave exit #3.
- 정문으로 들어오면 바로 체육관이 있어요.
  The gymnasium is right there once you enter the front gate (of a campus).
- 지금 신청하면 바로 받을 수 있을 거예요.
  You can have it right now if you apply.
- 114에 전화하면 전화번호를 바로 알 수 있어요.
  You can find out right away by dialing 114.
- 사진을 찍으면 바로 볼 수 있어요?   If I take a picture, can I see it right away?

**Practice**   Complete the dialogues, based on the example.

**Ex.**

A : 여기서 가까워요?

B : (나가다, 보이다)   나가면 바로 보여요.

1.   A : 책이 어디에 있어요?

B : (서랍을 열다, 있다) ______________________

2.   A : 신문이 어디에 있어요?

B : (문을 열다, 보이다) ______________________

3.   A : 사진이 언제 나와요?

B : (지금 찍다, 나오다) ______________________

○ 나가면 바로예요. 나가자마자 바로예요.  Right there, once you go out. Right there the moment you go out.

A way to say something is very nearby once you go outside.


○ A : 여기서 멀어요?  Is it far from here?

B : 아뇨, 바로 코 앞에 있어요.  No, it's right in front of your nose.

아뇨, 바로 코 앞이에요.  No, it's in front of your nose.

This means it's really close.


: Korean
Insight

# Korean Cartoon Characters 한국의 만화 캐릭터

Do you know who Dulli is? Dulli is a dinosaur. He is the creation of the cartoonist Kim Su-jeong, who in 1983 wrote the cartoon book Dulli, the Baby Dinosaur. The book was so popular they made it into a movie, and eventually even a musical. Dulli was perhaps one of the first Korean characters to get his own franchise product line. In 2003, the city of Bucheon, Gyeonggi Province, even made him an honorary citizen with his own Korean national identity card on the occasion of his twentieth birthday.

There are many other famous Korea cartoon characters, like Taekwon V, the main hero in Robot Taekwon V. He was recently signed over to one of the country's major entertainment management companies.

Others have followed Dulli as Korea's "character industry" develops, such as Masimaro, otherwise known as the "bizarre little rabbit," and the cute martial artist Ppukka. Among other things what these little characters have done is to show the world a different kind of image of Korea.

# 그런데 몇 번 출구로 나가요?

By the way, what number station exit should I go out of?

Track 059

## : Dialogue

**A** 그런데 몇 번 출구로 나가요?

**B** 잘 모르겠어요. 내려서 사람들한테 물어보세요.

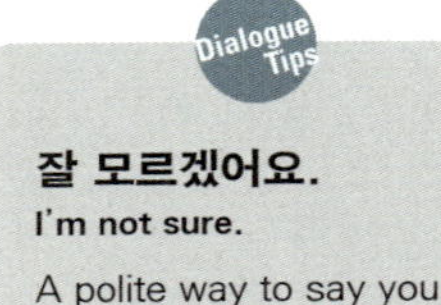

**잘 모르겠어요.**
I'm not sure.
A polite way to say you don't know something.

A  By the way, what number station exit should I go out of?
B  I'm not sure. How about asking someone after gettiing off?

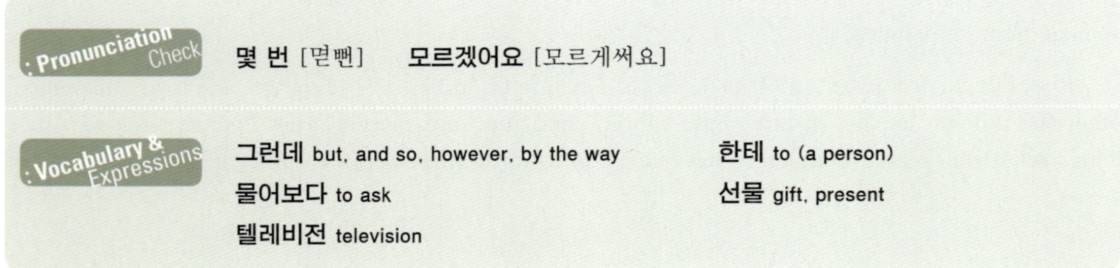

: Pronunciation Check

몇 번 [멷뻔]    모르겠어요 [모르게써요]

: Vocabulary & Expressions

그런데 but, and so, however, by the way        한테 to (a person)
물어보다 to ask        선물 gift, present
텔레비전 television

# V¹-아/어서 V²

Use this pattern to express chance or the unfolding of a process. V¹ and V² must be interrelated, and the result(s) the action that is V¹ influences V². This is not the same pattern as one that looks identical but that expresses the reason for something.

**그런데**

This either means something similar to the word "but" or is used to change the direction of a conversation. In this chapter we use it for its latter meaning.

- 집에 가서 점심 먹을 거예요.   I'm going to go home and eat.
- 교대역에서 내려서 3호선으로 갈아탈 거예요.

  I'm going to get off at Gyodae Station and transfer to Line #3.

- 선물을 사서 친구에게 주었어요.   I bought a gift and gave it to my friend.

★ If the verb stem ends in the vowels 'ㅏ' or 'ㅗ' use '-아서' and if it ends in anything else '-어서', the exception being if the verb is a '하다' verb, in which case say '-해서'.

- 만나다 → 만나서    운동하다 → 운동해서    읽다 → 읽어서

  **Make sentences, based on the example.**

**Ex.**
친구를 만나다 + 백화점에 가다

→ 친구를 만나서 백화점에 갔어요.

**1.** 집에 가다 + 텔레비전을 보다

→ ______________________

**2.** 선물을 사다 + 친구에게 주다

→ ______________________

**3.** 식당에 가다 + 밥을 먹다

→ ______________________

**4.** 체육관에 가다 + 운동하다

→ ______________________

**5.** 도서관에 가다 + 책을 빌리다

→ ______________________

- A : 지하철 타고 가세요.  Go by way of subway.

  B : 네. 그런데 요금이 얼마예요?  Okay. But how much is the fare?

- A : 다시 만나서 반가워요.  It's a pleasure to meet you again.

  B : 네, 저도 반가워요. 그런데 리사 씨는 왜 없어요?  I'm also pleased to see you. But why isn't Lisa here?

  Lisa was present the last time A and B met and so now that they meet again the direction of the conversation is changed from talking about being glad to see each other again to Lisa's absence.

- 질문 있으면 저한테 물어보세요.  Ask me if you have any questions.

  Use this to have someone ask you if there are any questions.



# Samgyeopsal 삼겹살

Samgyeopsal is one of Koreans' favorite dishes. Have you had the chance to try it? It's one of the more common choices if you eat out with your coworkers. These days it is becoming more popular than it had been for a while, and that has led to new ways of cooking it.

There is something called "wine samgyeopsal," in which wine is used to remove the birinnae, or the "scent of blood" from the meat and make it more tender. Then there's "yuja samgyeopsal," which is samgyeopsal that has the scent of citron (yuja). There's "plum samgyeopsal," "curry samgyeopsal," "herbal samgyeopsal," samgyeopsal with traditional health medicines, and samgyeopsal cooked together with tteok. Samgyeopsal is often a problem for the smell it creates, but these days people are developing a lot of ways to keep it from smelling up the room. Also, while most samgyeopsal establishments tend to be older restaurants, these days there are places that have designed their interiors to attract the younger generation.

# 남산에 가려면 어느 쪽으로 나가야 돼요?

## Which way do I have to exit to go to Namsan?

A  남산에 가려면 어느 쪽으로 나가야 돼요?
B  4번 출구요.
A  감사합니다.

A  Which way do I have to exit to go to Namsan?
B  Exit #4.
A  Thank you.

**감사합니다.** Thank you.
This is interchangeable with "고맙습니다.", but it would be good not to use this in its casual form, "감사해요."

남산에 [남사네]   어느 쪽으로 [어느쪼그로]

| | |
|---|---|
| 쪽 direction, side, way | 숟가락 spoon |
| 시험을 보다 to take a test | 열심히 enthusiastically, diligently, passionately |
| 동대문 시장 Dongdaemun Market | 끊다 to cut |
| 신다 to put on, wear (only for shoes, socks, other footwear) | |
| 신촌 Sinchon | |

# V¹-(으)려면 V²

An expression to be used when one has the intention of executing a given goal and is looking for a way to do so. If it is used in the imperative form, it is used to give the listener the advice he needs to succeed in carrying out his intention.



- 밥을 먹으려면 숟가락이 있어야 돼요.

  If I'm (you're) going to eat, I'll (you'll) need a spoon.

- 시험을 잘 보려면 지금부터 열심히 공부하세요.

  Start studying hard if you want to do well on the test.

- 옷을 싸게 사려면 동대문 시장에 가 보세요.　Go to Dongdaemun Market if you want to buy clothes cheaply.

★ If the final letter in a verb stem ends with a vowel, use '-려면'. Use '-으려면' if it ends in a consonant other than 'ㄹ', and '-려면' if it ends in a 'ㄹ'.

- 가다  →  가려면     끊다  →  끊으려면     만들다  →  만들려면

**Practice**　Complete the dialogues, based on the example.

**Ex.**

A : 백화점에 가고 싶어요.

B : (여기서 지하철을 타다) 백화점에 가려면 여기서 지하철을 타세요.

**1.** A : 옷을 싸게 사고 싶어요.

B : (동대문 시장에 가 보다) ____________________

**2.** A : 교수님을 만나야 돼요.

B : (여기서 기다리다) ____________________

**3.** A : 오래 걸어야 돼요.

B : (편한 신발을 신다) ____________________

**4.** A : 신촌에 가고 싶어요.

B : (여기서 버스를 타다) ____________________

- 백화점은 어느 쪽으로 가요?  Which way is the department store?

An expression for asking direction.

- 차를 싸게 사려면 이 번호로 전화해 보세요.  Here is the telephone number if you want to buy a car for cheap.

Use this pattern to give someone a phone number useful in achieving the initial speaker's intentions.

- A : 고속버스 타려면 어디로 가야 돼요?  Where do I have to go to catch an "express bus?"
- B : 이 길로 쭉 가면 돼요.  Continue along this way.

Expressions for asking and answering questions about directions.



# Mungyeongsaejae 문경새재

Korea's more famous tourist spots – places like Jeju Island and Mount Seorak – are certainly worth seeing. But much more of the country is just as beautiful. One such corner of the country would be Mungyeong Saejae, not as famous as Jeju and Mount Seorak, but it was the background for the television drama "Wang Geon."

The area is one of the great historical significance in that it was a main stop on the way to Seoul, back in the days when the capital was called "Hanyang," for young students on their way to take the state service exam during Joseon times. The scenery is beautiful and the nearby Suanbo hot springs make it a fine destination for families. You can also see the set for "Wang Geon," which adds to the curious things to be seen there. Traveling to see famous film and drama shooting locations has become a new trend in Korea these days. Why not take off on a "drama location trip" so that you have the pleasure of traveling while reminiscing about your favorite dramas.

# 왜 이렇게 늦었어요?

Why are you late?

**A** 왜 이렇게 늦었어요?

**B** 미안해요. 오래 기다렸죠?

A  Why are you late (like this)?
B  I'm sorry. You waited a long time, didn't you?

**Dialogue Tips**

**미안해요.** I'm sorry.

As this has an informal sentence ending it would be best to use it only with people who are close. Use "죄송합니다." with people you do not know or your elders.

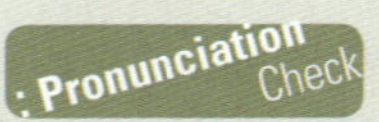

: **Pronunciation** Check

이렇게 [이러케]    늦었어요 [느저써요]    기다렸죠 [기다렫쪼]

: **Vocabulary & Expressions**

| | | |
|---|---|---|
| 이렇게 like this, in this way | 늦잠 oversleeping | 일찍 early |
| 밖 outside | 시끄럽다 to be noisy | 출근 to go to work (at an office) |
| 항상 always | 죄송합니다. I'm sorry. | |

## 왜 이렇게 A/V

A pattern for taking issue with a problem or view pertinent to the situation at hand. '그렇게' and '저렇게' can also be used, depending on what the dialogue refers to. The sentence ending '-지요?' may also be used with this pattern.

- 왜 이렇게 날씨가 덥죠? — Why is the weather so hot?
- 왜 이렇게 버스가 안 오죠? — Why is the bus not coming?

- A : 왜 이렇게 지하철에 사람이 많지요? — Why are there this many people on the subway?
- B : 출근 시간에는 항상 많아요. — There's always a lot during (morning) commute times.

- A : 왜 이렇게 늦었어요? — Why are you so late?
  B : 죄송합니다. 늦잠을 잤어요. — I'm sorry. I slept in.

- A : 수미 씨가 왜 저렇게 울어요? — Why is Sumy crying so?
  B : 시험에 떨어졌대요. — She says she failed the test.

 **Complete the dialogues, based on the example.**

**Ex.**
A : 날씨가 너무 더워요.

B : 왜 이렇게 날씨가 덥죠?

**1.** A : 이 구두는 너무 비싸요.

B : ___________

**2.** A : 비가 너무 많이 와요.

B : ___________

**3.** A : 지하철에 사람이 너무 많아요.

B : ___________

**4.** A : 바나나가 너무 맛이 없어요.

B : ___________

**5.** A : 밖이 너무 시끄러워요.

B : ___________

○ **왜 이렇게 비가 많이 오죠? 비가 왜 이렇게 많이 오죠?** Why is there this much rain? Why is it raining this much?

You can use these expressions when it's raining too much. The word order is different, but both mean the same thing.

○ **왜 그렇게 웃어요? 왜 이렇게 웃어요? 왜 저렇게 웃어요?**
Why are you laughing like that? Why are you laughing so? Why are you (is s/he) laughing like that?

An expression that can be directed to someone who is laughing excessively. The choice of '이렇게', '그렇게', and '저렇게' changes depending on the position of the speaker and listener.

# Taekwondo 태권도

If China has "Wushu" and Japan has "Karate", Korea has "Taekwondo." It used to be something enjoyed exclusively by men, but now a lot of women do taekwondo, too. It first began two thousand years ago as a uniquely developed Korean martial art and today is a globally recognized sport. Since the 27th Olympic Games in Sydney it has been an Olympic event as well.

As an excercise in which the whole body is used, taekwondo enables one to block an opponent's attacks using bare hands and feet. It involves using bare hands and feet to block an opponent's attacks. It is a philosophy of cultivating the body and mind to develop not only strong physical and mental strengths but also good judgment and confidence. Taekwondo, thus, leads the learners to be strong and gentle to the weak. The spirit of taekwondo is to be found in the attitude of integrity that comes from diligent practice. Why not learn taekwondo during your time in Korea?

# 온 지 이십 분쯤 됐어요.

It's been about twenty minutes since I came.

Track
062

: Dialogue

A  몇 시에 왔어요?

B  온 지 이십 분쯤 됐어요.

A  What time did you come?
B  It has been about twenty minutes since I came.

: Pronunciation Check

몇 시 [멷씨]    왔어요 [와써요]    이십 분쯤 [이십뿐쯤]    됐어요 [돼써요/뒈써요]

: Vocabulary & Expressions

개월 unit for number of months    승진하다 to be promoted, to promote

# V-(으)ㄴ 지(가) N이/가 됐어요

The particle is often omitted from this expression for explaining how much time elapsed between when an action was concluded to the present point in time. It cannot be used with an adjective and the sentence ending must always be in the past tense. When you want to ask, as a question, how much time transpired between when an action began to the present moment, use the expression 'V-(으)ㄴ 지(가) 얼마나 됐어요?'.

- 서울에 온 지 일 년 됐어요.　　It's been a year since I came to Seoul.
- 수영을 시작한 지 일주일쯤 됐어요.　　It has been about a week since I began swimming.
- 그 회사에서 일한 지 얼마나 됐어요?　　How long has it been since you began working at that company?

★　If the final letter in the verb stem ends in a vowel, use '-ㄴ지', if it ends with a consonant other than 'ㄹ', use '-은 지', and if it ends in a 'ㄹ', omit the 'ㄹ' and use '-ㄴ 지'.

- 가다　→　간 지　　　먹다　→　먹은 지　　　만들다　→　만든 지

# - 시간, - 일, - 주일, - 개월(- 달), - 년

These are units for describing how much time has passed. For '시간' and '달', use Korean numbers and for '일', '주일', '개월', and '년', use hanja (Chinese character) numbers.

- 한 시간, 삼 일, 이 주일, 육 개월(여섯 달), 일 년　One hour, three days, two weeks, six months, one year.

　Complete the dialogues, based on the example.

**Ex.**
A: 한국에 온 지 얼마나 됐어요?

B: 한국에 온 지 육 개월 됐어요.　(6개월)

**1.** A: 수영을 배운 지 얼마나 됐어요?

B: _______________________　(5년)

**2.** A: 한국어를 공부한 지 얼마나 됐어요?

B: _______________________　(3개월)

**3.** A: 승진한 지 얼마나 됐어요?

B: _______________________　(한 달)

**4.** A: 그 사람을 안 지 얼마나 됐어요?

B: _______________________　(2년)

**5.** A: 밥 먹은 지 얼마나 됐어요?

B: _______________________　(2시간)

- **한국어 공부를 시작한 지 얼마나 됐어요?** How long have you been studying Korean?

A way to ask someone who is studying Korean how long he has been studying Korean.

- A : **도착한 지 한참 됐어요?** Has it been long since you arrived?

  B : **아뇨, 별로 오래 되지 않았어요.** No, it hasn't been that long.

Question A is used when you want to know if someone arrived a long time ago. B is an answer to A, meaning that it hasn't been that long.

: Korean Insight

# Nurungji (Scorched Rice) 누룽지

Do you know what nurungji (누룽지) is? It's the tasty stuff that remains stuck to a pot rice has been cooked in and after the rice is done and removed. Back in the good old days when there wasn't much in the way of snack food, nurungji was enjoyed by all as a tasty way to satisfy the stomach. In homes that had a lot of children you might even have deliberately pressed rice against the side of the pot in order to make more of it than you might otherwise.

These days there are a variety of dishes that call for nurungji. There's a soup that has nurungji in it, crackers made from nurungji, candy that tastes like nurungji, and nurungji porridge. There are a lot of snack foods these days, but a lot of them have too much fat and sugar. Why not try nurungji, which doesn't have either?

# 어디부터 갈까요?

## Where should we go first?

**A** 우리 구경부터 해요.

**B** 좋아요. 어디부터 갈까요?

A   Let's start with sightseeing.
B   Okay. Where should we go first?

**Dialogue Tips**

**우리 구경부터 해요.**
**Let's start with sightseeing.**
Say this if you'd like to look around before you attend to other things.

**어디부터 갈까요?**
**Where should we go first?**
Ask this as you decide what you are going to see first.

**: Pronunciation** Check   좋아요 [조아요]

**: Vocabulary & Expressions**

구경 sightseeing   구경하다 to sightsee, watch   배고프다 to be hungry
손 hand(s)   씻다 to wash   설거지 dishwashing
청소 (room, house) cleaning

# N부터 V

An expression you can use to describe the order of one among various activities.



**A부터 B까지**

Here A is the starting point of something, but not necessarily the first in the order of something or a process.

- 남산부터 구경해요.  Let's see Namsan first.
- 어느 책부터 볼까요?  Which book should we read first?
- 배고파요. 밥부터 먹어요.  I'm hungry. Let's eat first.
- 집에 오면 손부터 씻으세요.  Wash your hands first when you come home.

- A : 뭐부터 할까요?  What should I do first/start with?
  B : 음, 설거지부터 하세요.  Umm, start by doing the dishes.

- A : 어디부터 갈까요?  Where should we go first?
  B : 도서관부터 가요.  Let's go to the library first.

- 설거지부터 청소까지 전부 다 해야 해요.  (You've/I've) got to do everything, from the dishes to housecleaning.

: Practice  **Complete the dialogues, based on the example.**

**Ex.**

A : 뭐부터 할까요?
B : 청소부터 해요.
〈청소〉

**1.**

A : 뭐부터 먹을까요?
B : ________________
〈김밥〉

**2.**

A : 어디부터 갈까요?
B : ________________
〈백화점〉

**3.**
A : 뭐부터 살까요?
B : ________________
〈우산〉

**4.**

A : 어디부터 갈까요?
B : ________________
〈극장〉

**5.**
A : 뭐부터 읽을까요?
B : ________________
〈소설책〉

○ **밥부터 먹고 합시다.**  Let's eat first (before doing the other things).

Say this if there are other things to do or concerns to attend to, but would like to proceed only after eating.

○ **어느 것부터 해요?**  What should I/we do first?

Say this when there are many things to be done, but you'd like to ask what should be done first. You may also say "뭐부터 해요?"

: Korean Insight

# The Four Seasons in Korea 한국의 봄, 여름, 가을, 겨울

Korea has four distinct seasons. Spring is full of freshness, when the weather turns warm and new sprouts begin to grow. In this season, Koreans begin farm work and the mountains and fields are full of flowers.

The mountains are particularly beautiful because many become covered in yellow forsythia and pink azalea. Summers are hot in Korea, but they are also lush season. Also, it is a time of abundant "summer fruits" like melons and watermelons. Autumn is a time when maple trees turn orange and yellow, giving the fields and mountains the coloring of fall. During this season people often go out of their way to visit mountainous areas known for their blushing autumn colors. In winter, the snow makes Korea's scenery more beautifully. As each of the four seasons passes, the spring comes again and a whole new year begins again.

# 064

# 여기서 사진 한 장 찍고 가요.

Let's take a picture here.

**: Dialogue**

A 여기서 사진 한 장 찍고 가요.

B 좋아요.

A Let's take a picture here (and then keep going on).
B Okay.

**Dialogue Tips**

**여기서 사진 한 장 찍고 가요.** Let's take a picture (and then keep going on).

Use this to suggest stopping to take a picture of an interesting or beautiful spot you come across in the course of sightseeing, before continuing on.

**: Pronunciation** Check

찍고 [찍꼬]

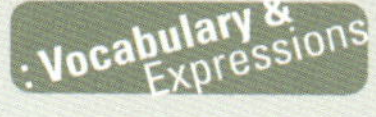

**: Vocabulary & Expressions**

장 unit for pictures, pieces of paper, etc
등산하다 to hike in the mountains, to go mountain climbing

# V¹-고 V²

A pattern for when the action in the preceding phrase is complete and now the next action is to be found in the latter phrase. There must not be a direct connection between the two phrases. This pattern can be used only with a verb, and the order cannot be reversed because V¹ has to reach completion before the sentence continues.

**A¹-고 A²**

A pattern that can also be used with adjectives, for sentences with phrases connected by what in English would be close to "and." There is no relation to time and sequence, so the order in which you introduce A¹ and A² are interchangeable.

Ex. 꽃이 싸고 예뻐요.
꽃이 예쁘고 싸요.

● 동생 만나고 도서관에 갔어요.

I met my younger sibling and then went to the library.

● 일요일 오후에는 등산하고 집에서 쉬었어요.

I went hiking Sunday afternoon then relaxed at home.

★ In contrast, here is another pattern in which the actions of V¹ and V² are interrelated. The action of V¹ or the result of its completion influences V².

● 친구를 만나서 영화를 봤어요.　　I met a friend and (we) saw a movie.

→ This sentence means you met the friend and then, with that friend, saw a movie.

● 친구를 만나고 영화를 봤어요.　　I met a friend and (then) saw a movie.

→ You met a friend, parted, and then saw a movie without that friend.

: Practice　　**Complete the dialogues, based on the example.**

**Ex.**　A : 주말에 뭐 할 거예요?

B : (친구 만나다 + 도서관에서 공부하다)　친구 만나고 도서관에서 공부할 거예요.

**1.**　A : 내일 뭐 할 거예요?

B : (운동하다 + 집에서 쉬다) ___________

**2.**　A : 저녁 언제 먹을 거예요?

B : (청소하다 + 저녁 먹다) ___________

**3.**　A : 언제 떠날 거예요?

B : (커피 마시다 + 떠나다) ___________

○ 밥만 먹고 올게요.  I'm just going out to eat, then I'll be back.

Something commonly said as you leave the house to eat out. It implies that you will not be gone very long.

○ 친구 만나고 올게요.  I'm going to meet a friend, then I'll be back.

A sentence that tells someone what you're going to do while out.

○ 이것만 끝내고 갈게요.  I'll go after finishing this.

A sentence that tells someone when you'll be leaving.

# Byeoljubu Jeon 별주부전

Have you ever heard of the old Korean story Byeoljubu Jeon? Every Korean knows it by heart. Once upon a time the Dragon King, who lived in the East Sea, was sick. He tried various medicinal remedies but to no avail. One day a doctor told him he would only get well after eating a rabbit's liver, so the king gathered his retainers to choose one to send to land for a rabbit liver, but they fought among themselves and were unable to decide who should go. Two of his retainers, an octopus and a snapping turtle, insisted on going to catch a rabbit but in the end it was the snapping turtle who got to go. Taking a drawing of what a rabbit looks like he went to land and found one in a gathering of land animals. The snapping turtle tricked the rabbit, telling him that life on land is dangerous and that happiness awaited him in Dragon Palace. Eventually the rabbit agreed to go, and rode into the sea upon the snapping turtle's back.

Upon arriving, however, the rabbit tricked the Dragon King's court by saying he had left his liver back on land, so back to land he went. The snapping turtle followed, but the rabbit ran off into the woods after teasing him while running around asking which beast of the wild had made off with his liver. The snapping turtle was terribly disappointed. He returned to the palace and no one knows what became of the Dragon King. No matter how dangerous a situation you're in, you should be able to find a way out of the bind you're in if you are as resourceful as the rabbit in Byeoljubu Jeon.

# 저, 사진 좀 찍어 주시겠어요?

Umm, would you please take my picture?

Track 065

**A** 저, 사진 좀 찍어 주시겠어요?
**B** 네. 웃으세요.

A Umm, would you please take my picture?
B Sure. Smile.

**Dialogue Tips**

저, 사진 좀 찍어 주시 겠어요? Umm, would you please take my picture?

A way to ask someone you do not know to take your picture for you.

---

**Pronunciation Check**

찍어 주시겠어요 [찌거주시게써요]    웃으세요 [우스세요]

**Vocabulary & Expressions**

웃다 to smile, laugh    돕다 to help    도와주다 to help
짐 luggage, bags    들다 to lift

208

## V-아/어 주시겠어요?

A very polite expression for asking a favor of someone. It is interrogative in terms of its form, but in actuality it is used like 'V-아/어 주세요' while being more polite.

- 좀 도와주시겠어요?    Might you be able to help me?
- 전화번호 좀 가르쳐 주시겠어요?  Would you kindly tell me your/the phone number?
- 신분증 좀 보여 주시겠어요?    Would you please show me some identification?

★ If the verb stem ends in 'ㅏ' or 'ㅗ', use '-아'. If the verb is a '하다' verb, the '하' of '하다' becomes '-해'. For all other verb stems, use '-어'.

- 오다 → 와 주시겠어요?
- 읽다 → 읽어 주시겠어요?
- 전화하다 → 전화해 주시겠어요?

**"저, ~"**

Something frequently said when first getting someone's attention, especially when you are interrupting. It is often used when you are about to speak and want to get the attention of those around you.



**Make the sentences below, based on the example.**

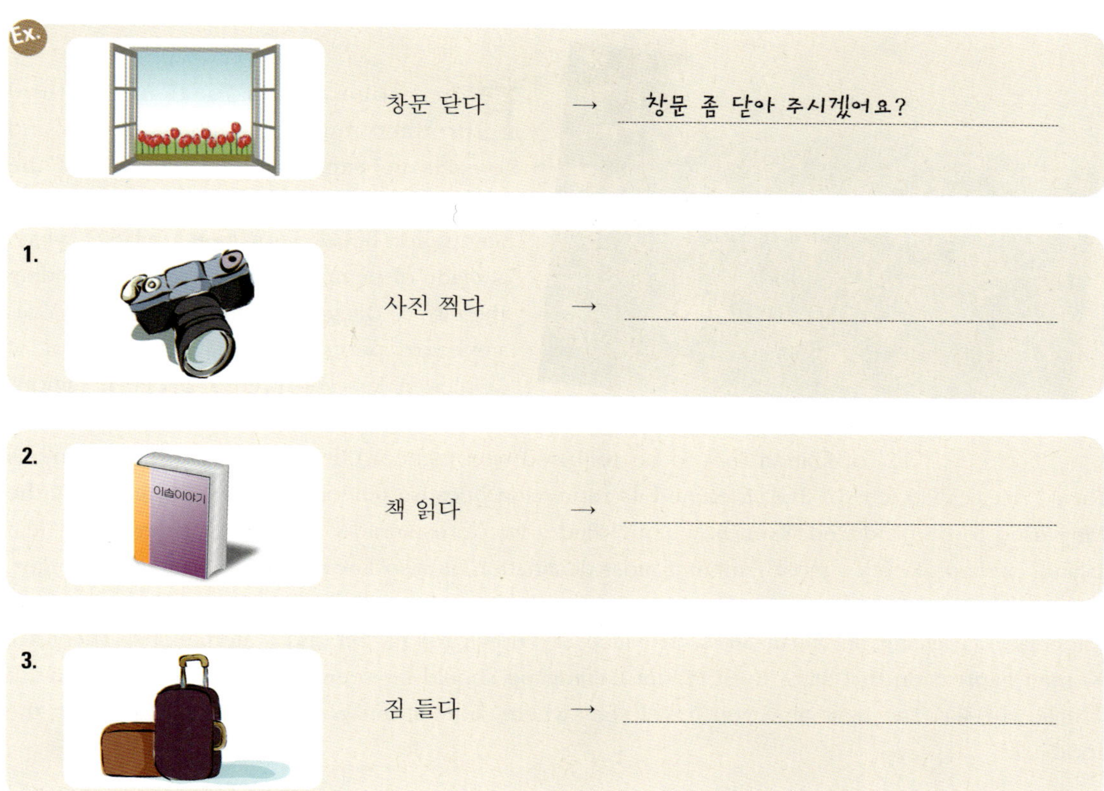

Ex. 창문 닫다 → 창문 좀 닫아 주시겠어요?

1. 사진 찍다 → _____________

2. 책 읽다 → _____________

3. 짐 들다 → _____________

209

- **"김치." 해 보세요.**  Say "kimchi".

  A way to tell people to smile. You are trying to be able to take a picture while people are still saying "chi." A Korean expression.

- **살짝만 더 웃으세요.**  Make your smile a little bigger.

  Say this when someone isn't smiling enough.

- **찍습니다, 하나, 둘, 셋!**  Here we go. ("I'm going to shot now") One, two, three!
  **찍어요, 하나, 둘, 셋!** Get ready ("I'm going to take the picture now"). One, two, three!

  Say this when you are about to take a picture of an individual or a group. Take the picture on "three."

: Korean Insight

# Korea's Diverse Local Products 한국의 다양한 특산물

Every country has local agricultural products unique to each region, and Korea is no exception. To the east of the Korean mainland is Ulleung Island, which is famous for hobak yeot (see Unit 52) which is made of pumpkin. The region surrounding the city of Daegu is famous for apples. You've heard people say that eating a lot of apples makes you pretty? Daegu is famous for having a lot of pretty women. The city of Icheon (not to be confused with Incheon), located near Seoul, is famous for its rice, called Icheon Ssal. It earned its reputation because Icheon is where rice eaten by the king used to be produced. Even now you'll find a lot of restaurants with good-tasting food. Jeju Island, perhaps Korea's most famous tourist destination, is also known for its mandarin oranges. If you go to Jeju you'll notice food products made from mandarin oranges such as jam and chocolate. Gochang, in North Jeolla province, is known for its eel and watermelons. There's a Korean expression that says, Even Mount Geumgang should be seen only after you've eaten (금강산도 식후경). The next time you travel somewhere, how about going for the scenery and the food?

210

# Appendix

### Unit 001 ...... p. 17

1. 저는 리사 켈리입니다.　　저는 미국 사람입니다.
　 저는 선생님입니다.
2. 저는 왕핑입니다.　　　저는 중국 사람입니다.
　 저는 회사원입니다.

### Unit 002 ...... p. 20

1. 제 우산입니다.
2. 제 책상입니다.
3. 제 가방입니다.

### Unit 003 ...... p. 23

1. 가요.
2. 와요.
3. 먹어요.
4. 봐요.
5. 마셔요.
6. 배워요.
7. 공부해요.
8. 운전해요.

### Unit 004 ...... p. 26

1. 저기는 화장실이에요.
2. 여기는 은행이에요.
3. 거기는 병원이에요.
4. 저는 학생이에요.
5. 리사는 미국 사람이에요.
6. 왕핑은 회사원이에요.

### Unit 005 ...... p. 29

1. 화장실이 어디예요?
2. 학교가 어디예요?
3. 집이 어디예요?
4. 식당이 어디예요?
5. 교회가 어디예요?

### Unit 006 ...... p. 32

1. A : 초콜릿 있어요?　B : 네, 있어요.
2. A : 우유 있어요?　　B : 아니요, 없어요.
3. A : 사과 있어요?　　B : 네, 있어요.

### Unit 007 ...... p. 35

1. A : 어디 있어요?　　B : 옆에 있어요.
2. A : 어디 있어요?　　B : 위에 있어요.

### Unit 008 ...... p. 38

1. A : 이거 얼마예요?　B : 이천오백 원이에요.
2. A : 이거 얼마예요?　B : 만천 원이에요.

### Unit 009 ...... p. 41

1. A : 저거 얼마예요?　B : 삼천 원이에요.
　 A : 이건 얼마예요?　B : 칠천이백 원이에요.
2. A : 물 얼마예요?　　B : 천 원이에요.
　 A : 껌은 얼마예요?　B : 오백 원이에요.
3. A : 우유 얼마예요?　B : 천오백 원이에요.
　 A : 빵은 얼마예요?　B : 오백 원이에요.

### Unit 010 ...... p. 44

1. A : 공책 한 권에 얼마예요? B : 팔백 원이에요.
　 A : 그럼 세 권 주세요.
2. A : 주스 한 잔에 얼마예요? B : 이천오백 원이에요.
　 A : 그럼 두 잔 주세요.

### Unit 011 ...... p. 47

1. A : 지금 몇 시예요?　B : 다섯 시 십오 분인데요.
　 A : 고맙습니다.
2. A : 지금 몇 시예요?　B : 아홉 시 삼십 분인데요.
　 A : 고맙습니다.

### Unit 012 ...... p. 50

1. A : 뭐 먹을까요?　　B : 사과 먹어요.
2. A : 몇 개 살까요?　　B : 두 개 사요.
3. A : 뭐 마실까요?　　B : 우유 마셔요.
4. A : 어디 갈까요?　　B : 도서관에 가요.

### Unit 013 ...... p. 53

1. A : 무슨 요일에 친구를 만나요?
　 B : 수요일에요. / 수요일요.
2. A : 무슨 요일에 영화를 봐요?
　 B : 일요일에요. / 일요일요.

### Unit 014 ...... p. 56

1. 일주일 전에 왔어요.
2. 삼 일 전에 갔어요.
3. 어제 갔어요.

### Unit 015 ...... p. 59

1. A : 어디에서 책을 읽었어요?　B : 도서관에서요.
2. A : 어디에서 밥을 먹었어요?　B : 식당에서요.

1. 컴퓨터 사러 쇼핑센터에 가요.
2. 친구 만나러 공항에 가요.
3. 영화 보러 극장에 가요.
4. 차 마시러 커피숍에 가요.
5. 책 빌리러 도서관에 가요.


1. 버스로 가요.
2. 오토바이로 왔어요.
3. 비행기로 갔어요.


1. 오늘 만날 수 있어요?
2. 내일 올 수 있어요?
3. 삼계탕 먹을 수 있어요?
4. 혼자 갈 수 있어요?
5. 읽을 수 있어요?


1. A : 집에서 공항까지 얼마나 걸려요?
   B : 두 시간쯤 걸려요.
2. A : 집에서 슈퍼까지 얼마나 걸려요?
   B : 삼십 분쯤 걸려요.
3. A : 집에서 경주까지 얼마나 걸려요?
   B : 다섯 시간쯤 걸려요.
4. A : 여기에서 저기까지 얼마나 걸려요?
   B : 이십오 분쯤 걸려요.
5. A : 한국에서 일본까지 얼마나 걸려요?
   B : 한 시간 삼십 분쯤 걸려요.


1. 물만 사면 돼요.
2. 극장 앞에서 만나면 돼요.
3. 5과까지 읽으면 돼요.
4. 저기서 타면 돼요.
5. 세 시에 가면 돼요.


1. 옷이 비싸면 안 살 거예요.
2. 영화가 재미있으면 또 볼 거예요.
3. 사과가 맛있으면 더 사러 갈 거예요.
4. 비가 오면 집에 있을 거예요.
5. 포도가 싸면 많이 살 거예요.


1. 거기 서울백화점이죠?

2. 거기 한국대학교죠?
3. 거기 중국집이죠?


1. 일곱 시인데요.
2. 금요일인데요.
3. 서울역인데요.


1. 거기 김 선생님 댁이죠?
   김 선생님 계시면 좀 바꿔 주세요.
2. 거기 김영 씨 집이죠?
   김영 씨 있으면 좀 바꿔 주세요.


1. 잘못 거셨어요.
2. 잘못 쓰셨어요.
3. 잘못 사셨어요.


1. A : 거기 2343-2344 아니에요?
   B : 아닌데요. 여기는 2343-2343이에요.
2. A : 거기 017-363-9807 아니에요?
   B : 아닌데요. 여기는 017-364-9807이에요.
3. A : 거기 02-889-5488 아니에요?
   B : 아닌데요. 여기는 02-880-5488이에요.


1. A : 리아 씨 부탁합니다.  B : 지금 식사 중이신데요.
2. A : 박 선생님 부탁합니다.  B : 지금 수업 중이신데요.
3. A : 김영 씨 부탁합니다.  B : 지금 샤워 중이신데요.


1. 이름은 왕핑이고요, 중국 사람이에요.
   회사원이고요, 전화번호는 2345-9876이에요.
2. 이름은 이수미고요, 한국 사람이에요.
   학생이고요, 전화번호는 3473-2079예요.


1. 운전하고 있는데요.
2. 신문 읽고 있는데요.


1. 못 가요.
2. 못 먹어요.
3. 못 받아요.
4. 못 봐요.
5. 못 놀아요.

## ㄷ





## ㄹ



## ㅁ